TOWARD CENTER

The Art of Being for Musicians, Actors, Dancers, and Teachers

Other Publications by James Jordan

Evoking Sound
Second Edition with DVD
(G-7359)

The Musician's Soul
(G-5095)

The Musician's Spirit
(G-5866)

The Musician's Walk
(G-6734)

The Anatomy of Conducting DVD
Architecture & Essentials: Choral and Instrumental
with Eugene Migliaro Corporon
(DVD-745)
Workbook (G-7358)

The Choral Rehearsal
Vol. 1: Techniques and Procedures (G-7128)
Vol. 2: Inward Bound–Philosophy and Score Preparation (G-7129)
The Choral Rehearsal DVD (DVD-720)

The Choral Warm-Up
(G-6397)
Accompanist Supplement, with accompaniment CD (G-6397A)
Modal Exercises, with accompaniment CD (G-6912)
Accompanied Canons for Choirs, with accompaniment CD (G-7145)
Index Card Pack (G-6397I)

The Choral Conductor's Aural Tutor
a companion to *The Choral Warm-Up*
(G-6905)

Listen! Introductory Harmonic Immersion Solfege
with Marilyn Shenenberger
(G-6971)

Ear Training Immersion Exercises for Choirs
(G-6429)

Choral Ensemble Intonation: Methods, Procedures, and Exercises
with Matthew Mehaffey
(G-5527T)
Teaching Procedures Video (VHS-500)

Evoking Sound DVD: Body Mapping Principles and Basic Conducting Techniques
with Heather Buchanan
(DVD-530)

Learn Conducting Technique with the Swiss Exercise Ball
(G-6478)

TOWARD CENTER

The Art of Being for Musicians, Actors,

Dancers, and Teachers

James Jordan

Nova Thomas

Foreword by James Conlon

GIA Publications, Inc.

Chicago

Toward Center

The Art of Being for Musicians, Actors, Dancer, and Teachers.

James Jordan and Nova Thomas

Art direction/design: Martha Chlipala

Photos pages 30 to 34 courtesy of James Caulfield and the Frank Lloyd Wright Preservation Trust

G-7661

ISBN: 978-1-57999-769-4

DEDICATION

To Leslie Jordan and Elizabeth Jordan
who have taught me Center by example

—James Jordan

To Mama, Muriel, Banks, Colin,
and Keith...my Center
And to my great teachers and students...
fine company to keep for the journey

—Nova Thomas

CONTENTS

Three

Four

Five

Six

Seven

Twelve

Thirteen

Fourteen

Fifteen

Sixteen

Seventeen

Eighteen

Nineteen

Twenty

Foreword

James Conlon

As all roads once led to Rome, the peak of mountain is accessible from all sides; the "center" of our spherical earth could be accessed, in theory, through any point of entry. *Toward Center: The Art of Being for Musicians, Actors, Dancers, and Teachers*, by James Jordan and Nova Thomas, provides one more such point of access to the creation and performance of art on an infinite surface. Its message and method merit serious reading and consideration.

In contemporary American society education has been increasingly seen as a passport to financial success. The "packaging" of promises and the illusions of wealth and celebrity from a "career" in the arts tell us more about the predominant values of our society than it does about the actual practice of any artistic discipline. Fame and fortune, the barometers of careerism, are not measuring rods for art nor their practitioners. Neither the word "career" nor "profession," which simply implies the sufficient mastery of an ability to justify financial recompense, is adequate or, in my mind, worthy of the immense power and importance of serious art. I view the artistic life, regardless of the medium, as "a way of life." As such, it necessitates a center of gravity, a binding magnetic force that draws all things to that center and provides a structure to perception and translation of life's phenomena into an artistic product.

That is why the *center* is the subject of this book—to provide one more glimpse into the infinite space of creation. Seeking it is as fundamental as it is unavoidable to the serious pursuits of the artistic life.

Dual forces must be harmonized in successful artistic expression: intuition and learning, intellect and feeling, discipline and inspiration, spiritual and material, passion and control. The list is long. A mechanic is expected to know his or her tools and how to wield them. In art, we want more than that, desiring at least an intellectual, metaphysical or spiritual dimension that surpasses the material. And yet, without the mastery of the technique of the required instruments, the entire spiritual layer is inaccessible. Yes, music "means" something, yet it simultaneously "means" no more than its notes, their harmonies, dissonances, counterpoints and rhythms.

The paradox of opposites starts with the material and the immaterial. The former must be mastered. Practicing scales and arpeggios, struggling with reeds, bows, breath control, intonation and rhythm are all fundamental and non-optional and require a center. Mastery of rhetoric, gesture and declamation are to the drama what a lithe, elastic and expressive body is to the dance. Entering the mystical, metaphysical, emotive intellectual sphere of music, theater and dance *is* its goal, but it cannot be accessed without the physical ability to do so.

The road for the performing artist, whose mission is not creative but *re*-creative, must begin and end with an egoless denial of self. In the first stages of technical practice, an agreement must be made to turn the physical self into an instrument. In the studying of the material of the art, the actual music, drama or dance "scenario," the full impact of the non-material, spiritual power of the art can only be grasped by humble, egoless study. To the degree the "interpreter" can empty himself or herself of the self, the essence and "self" of the music can infuse the soul of the potential interpreter. And then the egoless use of the body's instrumentality (serving the assumed essence of the music) is ready to transmit. The music, dance or drama must be used to communicate it all to those gathered to absorb the experience.

Dialectics, paradoxes, contradictions, material and spiritual forces, emotional and intellectual poles, disciplined and spontaneous performance are the stuff of the artistic life. Their coordination is not possible without a firm structure—the bones that support the organs, muscles and sinews. The head and heart cannot function without a unifying principle. That principle is to be found at the crossroads through which each element must pass. That crossroad stands at—and is—the center.

—James Conlon

The
eye is the first
circle; the horizon which it
forms is the second; and throughout
nature this primary figure is repeated
without end. It is the highest emblem in the
cipher of the world. St. Augustine described
the nature of God as a circle whose center
was everywhere, and its circumference
nowhere. We are all our lifetime
reading the copious sense of this
first of forms. (p. 133)[1]

—Ralph Waldo Emerson, Circles, Essay 1841
Essays and English Traits by Charles W. Eliot, Editor

1. Source http://www.bartleby/br/oo50.htm

TOWARD CENTER

Introduction
Toward Center: An Introduction

James Jordan

The mind and the body should have been granted natural faculties. That goes without saying. But with the gifts alone, one cannot go very far. It is important to remember that the greater the gifts, the greater must be the character, the power of the work, the conscience, the moral and spiritual value of him to whom they were given. I know "Unto every one that hath shall be given and he shall have abundance" (Matthew 25), but this is not achieved without great labor and patience. It cannot come without great love and great respect from the one who received. (p. 85)

—Nadia Boulanger
Master Teacher: Nadia Boulanger by Joseph Campbell

People say that what we're all seeking is a meaning for life. I don't think that's what we're really seeking. I think that what we are seeking is an experience of being alive, so that our life experiences on the purely physical plane will have resonances with our innermost being and reality, so that we actually feel the rapture of being alive. That's what it's all finally about… (pp. 4–5)

—Joseph Campbell
The Power of Myth

Well, and what is freedom? First of all, freedom seems to mean the absence of external restraint, the freedom to play. When we are free from external tyrannies, we seek freedom from our inner limitations. We find that in order to play we must be nimble and flexible and imaginative, we must be able to have fun, we must feel enjoyment, and sometimes long imprisonment has made us numb and sluggish. And then we find out that there are, paradoxically, disciplines which create in us capacities which allow us to seek our freedom. We learn how to rid ourselves of our boredom, our stiffness, our repressed anger, our anxiety. We become brighter, more energy flows through us, our limbs rise, our spirit comes alive in our tissues. (p. 22)

—Mary Caroline Richards
Centering

Yes, the highest things are beyond words.

That is probably why all art aspires to the condition of wordlessness. When literature works on you, it does so in silence, in your dreams, in your wordless moments. Good words enter you and become moods, become the quiet fabric of your being. Like music, like painting, literature, too, wants to transcend its primary condition and become something higher. Art wants to move into silence, into the emotional and spiritual conditions of the world. Statues become melodies, melodies become yearnings, yearnings become actions. (p. 11)

—Ben Okri
Art as a Way of Life
by Ann O'Shaughnessy and Roderick MacIver

An act of the self, that's what one must make. An act of the self, from me to you. From center to center. We must mean what we say, from our innermost heart to the outermost galaxy. Otherwise we are lost and dizzy in a maze of reflections. We carry light within us. There is no need merely to reflect. Others carry light within them. These lights must wake to each other. My face is real. Yours is. Let us find our way to our initiative. (p. 18)

—Mary Caroline Richards
Centering

A person's life purpose is nothing more than to rediscover, through the detours of art, or love, or passionate work, those one or two images in the presence of which his heart first opened. (p. 9)

—Albert Camus
Art as a Way of Life by Ann O'Shaughnessy and Roderick MacIver

To paraphrase a remark attributed to the revered conducting teacher Elizabeth Green, *you really haven't learned something until you have forgotten that you know it.* Most of use would recognize the truth in that statement. However, it was only recently, through a series of private lessons with graduate students, when the shocking realization came that the most central philosophical and physical concept guiding all of my conducting and musicing has become so "second nature" that I almost never discuss it, let alone teach it to my students! And so a bit embarrassed, I begin this journey with my colleague and friend Nova Thomas to try to describe this "thing" that has become so integral to my musicing and teaching.

Looking back on my conducting study with Elaine Brown, one of the most important concepts she taught me was *centering*. The first several months of study with her was spent exploring all the aspects of *Center* and just how important Center is to everything conducting. Her first assignments were to read three books: Mary Caroline Richards, *Centering in Pottery, Poetry and the Person*; Eugen Herrigel, *Zen in the Art of Archery*; and Martin Buber, *I and Thou*. For those who are familiar with my books, *The Musician's Soul* and *Evoking Sound*, you already know the central role these books have played in my thought. But only recently has the concept of Center been revealed as the core of what I do and, perhaps, what I am.

This book will provide ways that artists—musicians, dancers, actors, or for that matter, teachers—can explore the "how of being" while sharing their art in front of people. For each of us, doing serious and intense work "on" and "with" ourselves, coming to an understanding and awareness of our Center is central to the transmission of all things human. Center grounds and amplifies both our story and our message in the most direct and compelling human ways. Center is the way, perhaps the only way, by which we can both establish and maintain connection to other human beings and to ourselves. Without Center, conductors cannot communicate through meaningful gesture, singers cannot sing with a sound that compels, dancers cannot move with certain directness, and actors cannot create characters that connect with their audience.

There is no simple or easy explanation or description of what Center is. Perhaps the closest analogy in the psychological literature is the term *flow*, as Mihali Csikszentmihalyi has used it. *Flow* is that indescribable human energy that acts as the carrying medium for all meaningful human acts, which convey at their core our deepest desire to communicate. One's Center needs to be at the physical and spiritual core of all that we do. Energy "flows" in and out of us *through* Center.

An artist can acquire knowledge about and define the concept of Center, but the *acquisition* of Center is a small part of knowledge and a large part of life. Both Richards' *Centering* and Herrigel's *Zen in the Art of Archery* detail the slow, tedious, and demanding journey to a profoundly deep understanding and experience of Center. The purpose of this book is to guide each reader toward a gradual understanding of this deceptively simple term—a concept that is at the core of all great artistic expression.

Enso: Visual Symbolism of Center

The enso is perhaps the most common subject of Zen calligraphy. It symbolizes enlightenment, power, and the universe itself. It is a direct expression of thusness or this-moment-as-it-is. Enso is considered to be one of the most profound subjects in *zenga* (Zen-Inspired painting), and it is believed that the character of the artist is fully exposed in how she or he draws an enso. Only a person who is mentally and spiritually complete can draw a true one. Some artists practice drawing an enso daily as a spiritual exercise. (pp. xi–xii)

—Audrey Yoshiko Seo
Enso

The fascinating concept of *enso,* which is a character in Zen calligraphy, is a simple act of drawing a circle that carries with it tremendous symbolism. Enso is perhaps the best symbol for wedding the concept of Center, which this book is attempting to illuminate, with a spiritual and physical representation. Even the quality of the brushstroke portrays a living and organic shape. And the message of the enso is not only in its outside circle but also in its interior. The quality of the space in its Center determines the message of the enso.

Just as "only a person who is mentally and spiritually complete can draw" an honest and true enso, so it is with the artist. Honest and connected artistry, no matter the medium, is only possible when that communication comes through one's Center. Center is what makes us human. The presence of Center allows for the most direct and honest communication. When we perform and live through Center, we are moved to transcend the mundane life. Center is at the core of the fully human artist.

A friend and former student told of his experience completing a long fast. He undertook the fast as a last attempt at minimizing the debilitating effects of both asthma and a severe skin disorder. He spoke with considerable passion about how the fast had cleared his mind and how all symptoms of his physical maladies have since disappeared. In the almost ten years we had known each other, he never before had this level of energy nor the clarity that is now in his eyes. His fasting was a journey to re-establish Center, albeit a physical one. But that physical Center has had profound spiritual ramifications. Such intense work on Center can accomplish the very same thing for us as artists. It makes our intent clear and wipes away the ravages of human experience that cause us, even *make* us, to disconnect from the world with which we struggle to stay connected through our art.

Effects of Centering

The effects of centering on musicing, acting, and dancing are powerful and many. Musicing, acting, and dancing without Center make a difficult environment for creation and/or communication. Stated in positives, Center can have any or all of the following effects:

Center provides a physical grounding of one's energies,
which makes those energies strong, undiluted, and immediately
transferable to others.

Center provides a focal point for the artist's energies;
with such focus, those energies can be channeled at will to the
artistic task at hand.

Having a strong Center minimizes or eliminates tension, which
can cause multiple problems for artists.

Center provides the most direct line of communication from the
artist outward.

Honest and sincere artistry can only occur with centeredness.

Center allows for the correct use of the body. Center places the
artist at an anatomical advantage.

Constant awareness of one's Center enables the practice of all
things artistic.

Center has significant effect upon art when it is revealed to
others. The artist may have centeredness, but must want to both
connect and share that Center with others.

Center must be projected or propelled. Once the artist is
centered, it takes channeled energy to transmit the power of
that Center to others.

When the artist is truly centered, and that Center is grounded,
the artist usually feels as if he or she has "lost control." This feeling
of losing control to Center should be the goal for all artists.

So let us begin a slow and careful journey of understanding and
exploration. The suggestions and ideas presented here are intended to help
you on your journey to that place where humanness and artistic expression
live as one *within*: a clear vision of Center within (and without) the artist.
Be patient as you struggle with the complexity of this simple idea. Center is
both as simple and as complex as the enso. But without that understanding
through the deepest knowing, musicing will never achieve the composer's
intent, movement will never embody the message of the dance, and words
sung will never be able to connect with the human story to be told.

All of this notwithstanding, ultimately we should appreciate that the enso has no reason or point for its existence other than itself. It exists perfectly and completely, and is aesthetically gratifying for its own sake. The enso is its own merit and its own reward. It has no cause outside itself and provides no effect other than itself. The fruit of the enso is the enso. (p. xvi)

—Audrey Yoshiko Seo

Enso

Introduction

An Artist's Beginning

Nova Thomas

In order to share oneself honestly…, one must also have a center around which one's being holds forth. The word "center" is synonymous with many things, all of which form the core of a life and a person. A person's commitment to life, his awareness of the world around him, and his understanding of the beauty of the world and his own life are the foundation of a musician's center. It is out of this center that human impulse is channeled which, in turn, influences the pulse, musical line, and the color and textures…. But make no mistake about it, the conducting and creation of music flows from this thing called center. Center is the total integration of life and soul; inner being and outer being become one. (p. 10)

—James Jordan
The Musician's Soul

Art is simply a result of expression during right feeling…Any material will do. After all, the object is not to make art, but to be in the wonderful state which makes art inevitable. (p. 50)

—Robert Henri
The Art Spirit
Art as a Way of Life by Ann O'Shaughnessy and Roderick MacIver

Monkey Grows a Tail to the Center of the Earth

The need for Center, and in turn Centering, has long been accepted by most artists and athletes. Additionally, people in other occupations whose efforts and sensibilities require a bigger version of themselves and the role they play in this great theatrical event we call life understand the need for Center. Even our language is full of idiomatic phrases that refer to the problems of *not* being "there." Leonardo da Vinci, quoted by Michael Chekhov in *To the Actor, on the Technique of Acting* (Harper & Row, 1969) said, "The soul desires to dwell." This dwelling place of the soul is Center, and Center is our true "home." My cherished colleague and friend, James Jordan, has undertaken something important in writing this book. He has been most generous in inviting me to participate in this effort toward Center—in trusting me to contribute to this guidebook for *getting* there, *being* there and, ultimately, creating and communicating *from* there. I am grateful.

From the perspective and point of view of a performer, in fact an opera singer, it is a privilege to teach about what comes from what I have done (or tried to do) as a lyric storyteller. The challenge has been, and remains, to find a way to recognize, articulate, and share, through the wisdom of great teachers, the grace of experience and the blessing of "divine" instinct, what I *did*—at least on those "good" nights—in the theater. The journey continues. My wise father often said that our real challenge did *not* lie in the *achieving* of excellence in any particular endeavor, but in the *understanding* of it. That kind of understanding, that depth of work, I leave to James. The focus of my particular contributions is to illuminate a few fundamentals for the process— techniques for demystifying a *way*.

I am grateful to the many guides and traveling companions I've been blessed to encounter on my own journey toward Center. One of the most important of those companions was my wonderful Hallie, a beautiful, larger-than-life woman of Gullah heritage, who came to take care of my sister and me when Mama went to work. Hallie didn't need the skills of reading to tell great stories or quote the Bible, scripture and verse; she could cast spells and commune with the dead; and she knew secrets—real secrets—that could lead us back to Center. In moments when my sister and I were "misbehavin'," Hallie would simply and softly chant, "Monkey grows a tail to the center of the earth." We'd giggle and, oddly enough, get still. Hallie knew something about Center—she was a proprietress, a landlord of her Center and caretaker of ours. As for those of us who are mere mortals, well dear reader, we'll see each other along the way—buon viaggio!

One
Centering: An Artist's Dialogue with Silence

James Jordan

More often than not, we talk of things we scarcely know, we often discuss things of which we have no knowledge, and in reality we are often ignorant of things which we think we love. (p. 96)

—Nadia Boulanger
Master Teacher: Nadia Boulanger by Joseph Campbell

With all your science can you tell how it is, and whence it is that light comes into the soul?

—Henry David Thoreau

I read Spinoza's *Ethics* for the first time when I was thirteen years old. Of course at school we studied the Bible—which for me is the ultimate philosophical work. However, reading Spinoza opened up a new dimension for me, which is the reason for my continuing dedication to his works. . . .

This Spinozan brand of freedom is not a release from discipline
into arbitrariness of thought, but an active process. The more one
is able to determine one's own thoughts—in fact, causing one's
own thoughts, thereby creating one's own experience of reality—
the more it is possible to become self-determined and
to be truly free. (p. 37)

—Daniel Barenboim
Music Quickens Time

A true leader or musician leaves in others the conviction to
carry on. Can you get far enough away from
yourself to analyze yourself?

—Howard Swan
"Steps to Choral Excellence"
Lecture, July 1978

There is a common calling card for what Center feels like for us. It is a silent, comfortable and stabilizing place within. Many of us may not be familiar of the characteristic feeling of Center because we either have never experienced it or have lost the awareness of what it feels like to be in that "place." Center anchors and stabilizes not only us, but also our being.

It is possible to move through life without centeredness. While Center is not a requirement for living, it is certainly one of the things that make life meaningful. Being in center allows one to be aware at a new level. Center is a conduit for artistic expression, and for any artistic expression to be meaningful, it must come through the artist's Center.

A Description of Center

Artists, no matter their medium, may ascribe many descriptors to what can be referred to as Center. We artists know that when creative tasks have been fulfilled, there is a deep sense of contentment and utter stability that comes over us, even during performance. But what is more important, centeredness brings upon us a unique inner calm and utter inner silence. That silence seems to occupy a huge internal space when at its optimum presence. That silent spaciousness is a vessel, first and foremost for love and care—a kind of personal tabernacle of love for self and love for others—and for affirmation, both human and artistic. These characteristics are generally ascribed to an umbrella term, "energy." But Center is a place that is luminescent, brilliant, and strangely and utterly silent. That centered place, in addition to being silent, seems to be sheathed in humbleness.

All these qualities are described through words, a highly inefficient vehicle for things we know to be true if we have been made aware that they do actually exist within us. It is relatively easy for students to develop "outside" skills: rehearsal technique, conducting technique, and general musicing demeanor. However, it becomes profoundly difficult to take many of those students on an inward journey toward Center. There is something about the human spirit, one that has lived for a time in the world, which resists that journey—and many students struggle so to enter into such a journey. Life does complicate that journey and sometimes makes the inward journey more difficult, even convoluted. But artistry and profound human expression are never fully alive and present until that journey is made, a journey from head inward to one's deep heart core.

It may be that part, or most, of the resistance to that journey has to do with our inability to understand our innermost components; or perhaps it is because Center is a mixture of the bright and dark sides of our beings. When we journey inward toward Center, obstacles are encountered. At times, going inward is like entering one of those natural stalactite caves, where massive icicle-like growths seem to impose obstacles to going inward. We need to acknowledge that they are there and then navigate around them.

Silence brings with it an intense calm and, as Elaine Brown[2] (my teacher) used to call it, "rootedness." She always used to say that when we are centered, we feel a strong and intense connection downward, and that place, or the feeling of that place, would coincide with all the things in our lives that we most passionately believe in. She said that the signs indicating we are "in center" yield to us feelings that are rooted and strong, yet intensively silent, very internally spacious, and utterly calm.

Carlo Maria Giulini

Unfortunately, Center can only be learned through personal experiences that are wordless and in many ways mystical. Singing under the direction of Carlo Maria Giulini revealed more about centeredness and what Center is than any words can effectively accomplish in this volume. In reality, a person who is centered needs little gesture, if any, to convey sound on the podium. Perhaps conductors have the most difficult task because their ensembles are indeed "active reactors" to their Centers.

It was the opening of the Verdi Requiem. Giulini came to a piano rehearsal, mounted the podium, and stood there...still, calm...almost anchored. A small, almost imperceptible movement started the accompanist. On the surface, there was almost no movement, but it was apparent to all

---

2   Elaine Brown, Founder and Director of Philadelphia's legendary Singing City Choir, served as Director of Choral Activities at Temple University, Union Theological Seminary, The Juilliard School, and was Intern Conductor of the Westminster Choir.

present that there was an enormous amount of energy in the room coming from this man. When it was time for the choir to enter, we seemed to become one with Giulini. It may appear a bit fantastical to suggest, but we all felt that Center—a core of energy so profound and grounded that it spoke immediately to all in the choir—powerful simplicity that was honest and devoid of any ego. In Giulini's own words,

> My intention always has been to arrive at human contact without enforcing authority. A musician, after all, is not a military officer. What matters most is human contact. The great mystery of making music requires real friendship among those who work together. Every member of the orchestra knows I am with him and her in my heart.
>
> —Carlo Maria Giulini
> *"Carlos Maria Giulini quotes"*[3]
> *http://thinkexist.com/quotes/carlos_maria_giulini/*

So the great energy, what we are calling *Center*, which the choir felt that day, and in ensuing performances and rehearsals, can be described in yet another way. To be with others "in my heart"—this is probably the most profound and personal way of describing Center. While we must do our work (as described in later chapters) to anchor and stabilize our bodies, and then do the difficult work of opening our *selves* and our bodies to let breath inspirit us and open up our internal centers, it is perhaps the heart itself that transmits our human center, in all its complexity, to our students, ensembles, and audiences. Wordless, somewhat mystical and silent, it is this thing we call "Center" that changes moments and alters lives forever.

---

3 The misspelling of "Carlo" as "Carlos," as it is on this Web site, has been retained for ease of returning to the source of this quote.

Two
Inscape First

James Jordan

"Come sit down beside me,"
I said to myself,
And although it doesn't make sense,
I held my own hand
As a small sign of trust
And together I sat on the fence. (p. 1)

—Michael Leunig
"Sitting on the Fence"
Intimacy and Solitude by Stephanie Dowrick

You are all deep. It is the deepness of you I want to meet within
me. This may bore you, but I do not care because some year you
will remember, somehow. (p. 70)

—Nadia Boulanger
Master Teacher: Nadia Boulanger by Joseph Campbell

Those people who have a real sense of self have an inner reality, something virtually as precious as life itself because it markedly affects the ways in which you experience yourself and relate to others. A sense of inner reality gives someone, or maybe stems from, what Jung's colleague, Marie-Louise von Franz, called "solid ground inside oneself." (p. 8)

At just the time we need to treat ourselves with patience and compassion we strike the most painful blows against ourselves—from within. (p. 15)

It supports your awareness that you have a right to be alive in your own way, and that your relationship with yourself is more intimate and more knowledgeable than anyone else's experience of you can ever be. (p. 17)

People without memory do no have that sense of inner reality. They do not have self-acceptance. They are lost, until their memories can be found. Remembering who you are, you can largely take yourself for granted—you don't need to get up in the morning, look in the mirror, and ask your reflection who you are in order to get on with the day. (pp. 22–23)

—Stephanie Dowrick
Intimacy and Solitude

Life is art, for our social practices are embodiments of inner pictures and of inner feeling. Like art, life projects an inner world. What picture do we have of ourselves? Let us get to know the elements in ourselves which govern our choices. This is a lifetime's artistic labor: not to be gripped by faceless powers, but to see face to face whom we serve. (p. 138)

Art is then a process of transmutation, awakening an inner realm within the countenance of matter.

This was the old alchemists' art in the middle ages: to awaken the gold that lay in the depths of dung and red earth. This was not worldly gold, as they so often explained, but a gold of the spirit, warm radiant and incorruptible. The elements transforming in the crucible were agencies of transformation in the men themselves. The goal was the sacred marriage of the elements, and the birth of a new being, the homunculus, the new man. (p. 180)

—Mary Caroline Richards
The Crossing Point

Who's living in you? It's pretty horrifying when you come to know that. You think you are free, but there probably isn't a gesture, a thought, an emotion, an attitude, a belief in you that isn't coming from someone else. (p. 45)

—Anthony de Mello
Awareness

The necessary thing is after all but this: solitude, great inner solitude. Going-into-oneself and for hours meeting no one—this one must be able to obtain. To be solitary, the way one was solitary as a child, when the grownups went around involved with things that seemed important and big because they themselves looked so busy and because one comprehended nothing of their doings.

And when one day one perceives that their occupations are paltry, their professions petrified and no longer linked with the living, why not then continue to look like a child upon it all as upon something unfamiliar, from out of the depth of one's own world, out of the expanse of one's own solitude, which is itself work and status and vocation? Why want to exchange a child's wise incomprehension for defensiveness and disdain, since incomprehension is after all being alone, while defensiveness and disdain are a sharing in that from which one wants by these means to keep apart. (pp. 45–46)

—Rainer Maria Rilke

Letters to a Young Poet

Take a Gumdrop

Only years later have I begun to understand what my teachers tried so desperately to teach me when I was young. My third grade teacher, Sarah Farley, always kept a tree in our classroom. All over that tree, located at the back of the room, out of sight yet always in our awareness, Mrs. Farley placed fresh gumdrops every day. We would walk into school each morning and that tree had seemingly replenished itself with a new supply of fresh gumdrops.

We were told from the first day of school that we could go to that tree and take one gumdrop if we met one of two criteria. Those criteria, according to Mrs. Farley, began with sharing. If we did something kind for someone else, our reward was a gumdrop. We could also take a gumdrop if we were kind to ourselves in some way. Mrs. Farley explained that "while it is a great thing to share with others, do not forget to be kind to yourself." As a third grader struggling with that concept for several weeks, I remember thinking, "What does she mean, being kind to myself…that's silly." How can you be kind to *yourself?* This third grader could just barely wrap his head around the idea.

Well, it wasn't long before I began to figure out what it meant to be kind to myself. Each school day began with a math quiz. When we came into the classroom, the daily math problems were on the board. On one particular day, for some reason I did very poorly on the test. When I received my paper back after recess, a big D was at the top of the paper. I had never received a C, let alone a D. Panic set in and tears started to flow. At the same time, there was a tap on my shoulder. Mrs. Farley said, "James, you need to go take a gumdrop…be kind to yourself. It's not that important…you'll do better tomorrow."

A great weight had been lifted from my shoulders. But oh, the genius of that woman! What a clever way to ease a youngster into the importance of not only knowing himself but also being kind to himself. Sarah Farley was an "inscape artist." Through that gumdrop tree and reward system, she very gently started each of us on an inward journey—the important mission toward achieving self-awareness. She was such a clever teacher, for she had figured out a way to get young people to become aware of their "inscapes." It's also remarkable that, after all these years, I have not forgotten that gumdrop tree. In retrospect, how amazing it was that a teacher could set up a situation where children could stay in touch with others and themselves every minute they were in the classroom. In fact, this was the most important objective of Mrs. Farley's classroom. What a gift to give to children!

The Need for Inscape

Before any of us can speak about the miracles of centering, we must realize that Center is exactly that, a center, a core. That core can only become present through a certain type of ongoing awareness that *this is* the place where you live. The term *inscape* is a word from the poetry of Gerard Manley Hopkins, and it is perfect for beginning to approach a description of the inner life of an artist, musician, actor, or dancer.

First, one needs to be aware that inner space actually does exist. An artist also needs to understand that to be musical or creative, and if musicing is to be honest *and* communicative, that inner space must exist. That space, when present, is large and expansive. The upper body feels cylindrical, large, incredibly buoyant, and immensely spacious. At times, acquiring such an interior space requires us to do some work on our inner selves to enable that spaciousness to return. This inscape is a natural condition of human beings, especially those involved with creative acts. Finding ways to go into that space on our own, within our selves, seems to be important stuff for both artists and teachers.

It is deeply troubling, especially in music education, that "isms" and philosophies imbued with social injustice and discrimination are used to provide the core of why music is important. While such objectives are noble and thought provoking, honest music making and the miracle of musicing will never be taught or communicated if journeys into the inscape are not taken. Artists need their individual inscape to communicate their vision. They need this large internal space where words and music can resonate through them and out again. That space can only be attained by a simple, yet powerful technique: the awareness that it does, in fact, exist!

While Center (which will be dealt with in more detail in due order) is important to honest music making, it is this incredible interior spaciousness that houses both our spirit and our breath. Breath and spirit cohabitate this imaginary, yet very real, kinesthetic feeling within our bodies. The feeling of being spacious allows us to make that journey towards an understanding of Center. It must be a journey *down* and *in* that makes us aware that in the same instant we are simultaneously alive and caring beings.

The Potter

Perhaps the following story will shed some light on the concept above. Several years ago I attended a high-end craft show, a juried show in Sedona, Arizona. This was an exhibition of works by artists and artisans who clearly operate at the highest levels of artistry. For some reason that day, I decided to focus on potters. While all the pottery was beautiful, I came upon one booth where the pottery was not only beautiful but also expensive. So I asked the potter why his pottery warranted such high prices.

Luckily for me, he was not offended but instead, smiling, he said, "Let me teach you something about pottery." He began by saying that while many pots appear beautiful on the outside, the true work of art is on the *inside*. He explained that the interior space of the pot should be the same identical space as the exterior of the pot. And, for him, it was the interior space of the pot that defined its aesthetic beauty. He expressed that the pot's "spiritual" quality is contained in its interior space, not its external worldly appearance. As I ran my fingers inside his pots, it was probably the first time I had tactilely experienced spaciousness and a true sense of interiority. His pots were some of the most beautiful interior spaces I had ever touched.

When conducting, or even teaching, I try to envision within what my fingers taught me that day. It is odd, but now I am always aware of a person, especially a musician, who is "interiorly spacious." Those people have an unmistakable presence, and yes, even a radiance. It has become clear that very little musicing can happen unless that kind of interiority is present for others to experience. To gain the interior "air" of a pot takes first an awareness that it can and does exist within us, followed by a willingness to explore all those things that will cause our interior spaces to open.

Frank Lloyd Wright and the Physical Representation of "Inscape"

Just about everyone knows the name of American architect Frank Lloyd Wright. Many of us can recognize his distinctive exterior architectural style. From Scottsdale, Arizona, to Oak Park, Illinois, Wright's vision of what architecture could and should do lives on in his incredible structures that have been built all across America.

The first Wright building I experienced was Fallingwater, located outside of Pittsburgh, Pennsylvania. During that tour one summer, I was impressed with the beauty of the exterior, but I was more affected by the interior! The inside of the house had very low ceilings, but somehow the place seemed spacious. Initially it appeared to be a clever architectural optical illusion, but soon I was convinced otherwise. Through a brilliant alchemy of glasswork, woodwork that led the eye upward, and an astute use of color, after a few minutes I realized that the rooms were not only *physically* spacious, but they also *felt* incredibly spacious. Despite short ceilings and narrow hallways and passageways, this was the most spacious of spaces!

Years later, I stayed in a Wright-designed home of friends—what a thrill! On this first of many visits, I woke up early and decided to walk around the house. Once again, the sense of interior spaciousness was striking, but this time I understood a bit more what I was seeing. Everywhere as far as the eye could see, Wright's architecture, with an exterior beauty all its own, conveyed that miracle of interiors that gives the inhabitant a sense of space—of spaciousness—and being inside a spacious place. The vertical lines that permeate the design seemed to draw the eye upward and "into" the spaciousness of the house. This spaciousness evoked an incredible sense of interior space that in a magical way translated into the viewer's *own* interior "feelings." Great architects not only understand the exteriors of the buildings that they create, they also understand the power and symbolism of interior spaces. The lines of the windows seemed to make the outside world seem more spacious. Even the furniture had lines that contributed to this feeling of spaciousness, balance, and peaceful "interiority." I was so excited by what I saw; I ran to get my camera.[4] So yes, Wright understood inscape!

Freedom is from within.

—Frank Lloyd Wright

---

4   These photos are used with the permission of the homeowners.

No house should ever be on a hill or on anything.

It should be of the hill.

Belonging to it.

Hill and house should live together each the happier for the other.

—Frank Lloyd Wright

Form follows function—that has been misunderstood.
Form and function should be one, joined in a spiritual union.

—Frank Lloyd Wright

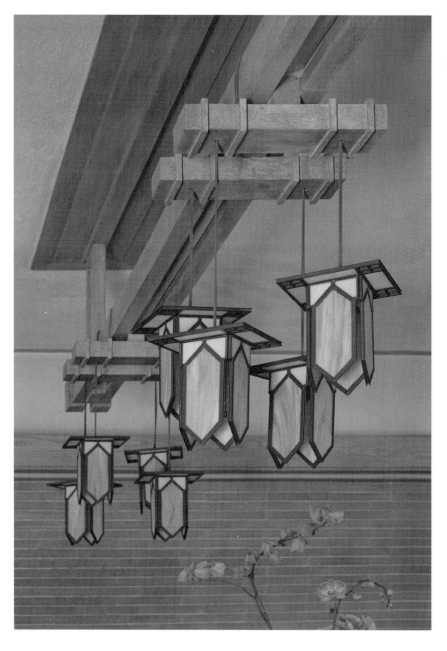

Space is the breath of art.

—Frank Lloyd Wright

Simplicity and repose
are the qualities that measure the true value of any work of art.
—Frank Lloyd Wright

Less is only more where more is no good.

—Frank Lloyd Wright

Get the habit of analysis—
analysis will in time enable synthesis to become your habit of mind.
—Frank Lloyd Wright

These understandings may lead you to a physical/psychological representation of what every artist's interior must be. St. Teresa of Avila described one's soul as a great "interior castle" with many rooms. No matter the analogy or the image, it is important for every artist, musician, and teacher to have a clear idea of his or her interior and how to access it "on demand." This process can begin with a visual conception and an experience of spaciousness. The awareness and conceptualization of that spaciousness makes the artistic acquisition of that spaciousness in times of musicing and teaching all that much easier. The ability to "call up" interior spaciousness will allow for a cascading of reactive responses within our being and within those who experience our art. Inscaping is the vehicle by which our honesty and connection to ourselves, and consequently with others, can take flight.

Three
The Journey Inward: Relaxation that Moves Us through "Neutral" to "Ready"

Nova Thomas

The "journey inward" can be a daunting one. It requires time, curiosity, will, and courage. And rarely is the terrain for this travel easily navigated. In fact it seems, more often than not, to be a proverbial jungle in there—or at least along the way to *there*. So I begin as most artists, and teachers of artists, do—with suggestions for clearing the clutter in the path, with *relaxation*.

There are many highly effective techniques for relaxation. The one that is "right" is simply the one that is right for you…the one that achieves the desired "un-cluttering." Since we are best served by clearly identifying the actual *goal* of any exercise, let us consider what it is we actually wish to accomplish through relaxation. Keith Buhl, Christopher Arneson, and I co-authored a curriculum of voice and speech study for the Actors Studio Drama School at the New School University in New York City (*Voice and Speech for the Stanislavsky Actor: A Curriculum Manual for Teachers*). In this curriculum we chose to use the term *neutral* as a way of describing the first desired result of relaxation. We devised a plan of action that moved the student and performer from exercises in relaxation through a place of neutral…a place of quiet and/ or still…to Center. We offered, as do most techniques, several exercises for getting there; but again, defining our goal was the first effort: "the release of those unnecessary tensions that impede the mind, body, and spirit of free release."

In acting we often reference the given circumstances of a particular scene or character—those situational influences that affect the meaning and state of being of any character. We, as characters in our own play, more commonly known as "our life," are operating constantly under various states of given circumstances—and they are almost always inappropriate for the artistic task at hand and the work we need to do. So perhaps our process for relaxation should begin with the recognition and identification of those physical, mental, and spiritual given circumstances that can potentially hijack free expression.

The following is a classroom exercise for achieving a physical state of neutral. We begin by methodically locating and identifying the tension, and then releasing it.

Body Scan—Recognition and Release

- Begin by lying on the floor, on your back, with knees up and slightly bent, and feet on the floor, eyes closed.

- Using a very specific rhythmic pattern of inhaling and exhaling, perform a basic "body scan" as the guide for recognizing and releasing tensions.

- Inhale to a count of four, creating an awareness of any tension there may be in a specific part of your body (e.g., the feet and/ or ankles).

- On an exhalation of four, move that part of the body and release the tension.

- Continue this simple pattern of inhalation and exhalation to steady counts of four as you travel through the body: knees, thighs, hips, waist, chest, arms, hands, shoulders, neck, face and head. *Again, the inhalation visits the target of focus, and the exhalation consciously releases any identified tenseness.*

Note:
Keep the assigned rhythmic pattern of breathing steady. We are rhythmic creatures. As forced or contrived as it may initially seem, rhythm is ultimately freeing.

"breathe"

"exhale and inhale" (both characters together)

As Bella Merlin elaborates on the teachings of Konstantin Stanislavsky in *The Complete Stanislavsky Toolkit,* "respiration plus rhythm form the foundations of all your creative work...Breath + Rhythm = Emotion." (p. 34)

Once the body scan is completed, simply "hang out" in this physical state of being—this physical state of neutral. Keep your awareness on your breath.

mushin

mu =
nothingness

shin =
heart; mind; spirit

The psychophysical connection is undeniable. Many argue that physical work is a gateway to mental and emotional achievement. But physical work is not enough; it is still necessary to devote specific time and exercise to that ever-looming challenge of "un-cluttering" the mind. Of course, entire practices are dedicated to this effort—of which meditation, visualization, prayer, and yoga are but a few. Once again, the right method is simply the one that is right for you—the one that achieves the desired state of neutral. In an exercise that parallels the physical recognition and release defined above, once again we call upon rhythm and breath to identify and release the given circumstances that cause impeding thoughts and mental clutter.

Recognition and Release for the Mind

- Find a comfortable position either seated or lying down.

- Using a very specific rhythmic pattern of inhaling and exhaling, perform a basic "mental scan" as the guide for recognizing and releasing tensions.

- On an inhalation to the count of four, identify *one* thought at the time—name it, and be specific.

- On an exhalation to the count of four, release that thought... let it go.

- Without pause or judgment, move to the next inhalation—the next thought—and continue the process of identifying and releasing.

- Note: Don't be distracted by judgments about whether or not you've been successful in releasing the identified thoughts. If they remain, simply go back to them and repeat the process. Once again, keep the assigned rhythmic pattern for the exercise steady.

These are just two simple exercises; there are countless others. The goal is to achieve a general state of neutral—a relaxed mental and physical state of being. Mary Caroline Richards, in *Centering: In Pottery, Poetry, and the Person*, refers to "external tyrannies." Tensions, whether physical or mental, are just that, and any movement toward Center requires, or is at least greatly benefited by, a cleared pathway.

Performance as an Event

But the process is not over. Relaxation, especially viewed as an un-cluttering gesture, is necessary for the movement *toward* Center; but for the movement *from* Center, the *expression*, we need another important preparatory step—a way for "ramping up." One cannot go to the stage merely relaxed; a relaxed state (at least as relaxation is traditionally understood) is not the terminal need or expression of a technical process that must ready us for the heightened needs of performing. Many students and young performers exhibit this confusion. Performing is an event that requires fire and focus. We should enter the scene (whether that scene be a concert hall, a stage, or a classroom) "on," ready to leap—not ready to drift into sleep. As a teacher, I often watch my actors from backstage. In beginning efforts, time after time, and at that crucial moment before the first footfall onto the stage, the actor shakes his or her body in an effort to "un-do." The rising energy or fire that was just seconds ago in place and ready to "leap" slows from a roar to a flicker…eyes dull, breathing slows, and a now more "comfortable" student meanders into a moment of the character's life or play. This is clearly not the goal. If we can once again reference the actor's process of identifying and participating in the given circumstances of character and play, we can create a through-line of preparation, to use terms coined by Don Greene (the renowned sports psychologist and performance coach), by "centering down" and then "centering up"!

The relaxation exercises methodically identify the current and given circumstances of our physical and mental selves. We then release the impeding clutter and arrive at a place of neutral. After we allow ourselves to hang out for a few moments in an uncluttered body and mind, then what? We need to engage in a process that, with the same method and measure we used in "centering down," invites the given circumstances required for the task at hand. This process tackles two avenues of responsibility. First, we must (again with specific goals in mind) "center up" to meet the technical needs of performing well—there must be a sort of *conjuring* and calling up of our craft. We should replace the unwanted tensions with an appropriate energy, or fire, for the *release* our performances require—the energy and intention to *launch* in that all-important moment between impulse and action. For example, I am very aware of my technical needs—the kind of energy, focus, and *tuning* my own instrument requires to resonate in the spaces and situations I inhabit as an operatic heroine. I know what I must *do* and what I must *think* (or be conscious of). It is important to be methodical and specific in this "centering up." So often, when left to our own undisciplined devices, we will randomly stab at individual steps in our process rather than methodically and consciously move through an order of events that organically summon and ready the instrument for the task at hand.

My own work finds its origin in the physical and mental before it moves to the vocal; I "light the fire" and focus the energy in the body and mind before I move to sound. Only after body and mind are readied do I proceed. Vocally, I have a specific warm-up that proceeds through unformed releases of sounds and primal moans to the refined and aesthetic needs of range, registration, dynamic vitality, and musical expression. Then, in a *shorthand* fashion, I review the mental prompts needed at crucial moments in the score.

After the "craftsman" is prepared, we then must turn to that second avenue of responsibility—all that has been readied must now be offered and yielded to the given circumstances of character and play. The fired and focused physical life becomes the architecture and shape of the character; the voice avails itself to the music of the score and the words of the script; and the mind becomes a dwelling place for the thoughts of the character. It is important to know that the performer is responsible not merely for producing the page, but for *occasioning* the need for the expression…be that musical, textual, emotional, or physical. In those moments when we feel that the word is there because the character needs to say it…that the music is there because the character needs it to express some heightened emotional state…or that the movement is there because a character needs to go somewhere and/or physically describe something—then authenticity is ours.

In summary, relaxation should move us from and through the clutter of our own given circumstances toward Center. We should allow ourselves to simply exist for a moment in this place of neutral; then with a determined, focused, and specific process, "center up" and offer a well-prepared instrument to the given circumstances of the character and play.

Four
The Wisdom of Melancholy:
The Anchoring of Center

James Jordan

Thus, the story of Adam and Eve is not about sin, disobedience, sex, or shame, but is an attempt to explain the reality of death. The first lesson in this tradition having to do with living the good life is that life, however good, is finite, a limited resource, and that one does not have all the time in the world to discover what it is or how to live it. The first duty of self-awareness, therefore, is the knowledge of the fewness of one's days. (p. 136)

—Peter Gomes
The Good Life

We may be able to say no, if we decide to feed our mind on presumption and conceit, to cling to duplicity and to refuse to mean what we sense, to think what we feel. But there is no man who is not shaken for an instant by the eternal. (p. 9)
Man is a messenger who forgot the message. (p. 43)

—Abraham Joshua Heschel
I Asked for Wonder

Life itself both defines and deepens Center. Jan Swafford, in his book *Johannes Brahms: A Biography*, remarked in the concluding chapter that a great composer has the ability to cause one to contemplate one's end. He makes the point that one of the remarkable aspects of Brahms' music is its ability to force one to look backward with a certain kind of life wisdom and melancholy. It is this "backward melancholia" that gives the music of Brahms its great life-changing gravitas. And it is almost impossible to make the journey

Note:

A Native American Medician Man symbol resembling an eye, also represents wisdom and awareness.

Perhaps not so much an eye looking backward or looking forward, but from the center, looking out.

with Brahms if one cannot access one's Center through both breath and belief in the message contained within that music. Composers also use musical devices as symbols of looking backward—for the best music seems timeless, the way it's always been. How does it do that? By forcing the human spirit to not only look backward, but also to acknowledge the brevity of one's life. Lance Armstrong talks about how his life changed (for the better) with his cancer diagnosis.

Great composers have this uncanny ability to "see backward," to teach us about life in the rearview mirror. On a video recording of Robert Shaw leading a choral workshop,[5] a participant posed the following question: "Do you not believe, Mr. Shaw, that the Crucifixus of the B minor mass of Bach is the greatest musical depiction of the crucifixion of Christ known to music?" Mr. Shaw replied, in effect, that the Crucifixus of the Mass in B Minor is not programmatic. What makes that

5 *Carnegie Hall Presents Robert Shaw: Preparing a Masterpiece, Part I (A Choral Workshop on Brahms' A German Requiem.* VHS Carnegie Hall Corporation.

music so profound is that Bach understood the enormity of the event and its effect upon all of mankind.

Many of the great musicians I have known, or known by reputation, have had experiences that have not only created Center, but also anchored it profoundly and deeply. Elaine Brown, one of the most centered people I have ever known, endured the murder of her husband and the death of her daughter. She often remarked that life "makes us stronger." I would like to paraphrase and say that life "grants us Center." Itzhak Perlman's disability has certainly centered not only his life but also his musicing. The great baritone Thomas Quasthoff, crippled by the drug thalidomide given to his mother in pregnancy, is one of the great examples of an artist who knows Center. It is remarkable to consider this great artist: there should be no reason why he is able to sing the way he sings. His body looks as if it might be incapable of producing and supporting a sound. But sing he does! As you listen to Quasthoff sing, you are touched from his Center to yours. His Center is so strong and compelling it pulls your ear and spirit along with him. And likely it is because of his Center that he sings.

Note:

These multiple crosses are an alchemical symbol representing the levels of increased awareness, also called the ladder of the soul, representing the soul's journey through existence ending in paradise.

What Bach brought to the Mass in B Minor, and every other piece he wrote, was his awareness of the world and of life. No one would argue that Brahms brought his unique viewpoint of life to his music, in a type of aware melancholia, to give his listeners the ability to look backward in life to see with sharp awareness the complexity of human existence. Both composers must have written while in a state of incredible awareness of not only themselves, but also the human condition that they constantly inhabited.

One aspect of Center seems to be hewed out of our deepest interior space by life itself. The great preacher William Sloan Coffin once wrote that until one makes the journey from "head to heart," we really cannot know Center. One aspect of Center is that it is a space created deep within us by our experiences in life itself, and this aspect is anchored by the realization and re-realization that our time here is only so long. Such melancholy gives a profound gravitas to our Center as artists and persons. While we all possess Center to some degree, the challenge is to anchor that Center deeply within us. It is life itself that allows us to drop that Center lower within ourselves, forming one important aspect of Center.

Five

Manifesting the Journey Inward: Outward Expression

Nova Thomas

For better or worse, I am one of those goal-oriented people. While there is a great art to *being*, that state must ultimately find its expression and worth in *doing*. Now, doing without reason, without some authentic origin or Center, is merely random activity. But *doing* from a centered and decent place of *being*, would be the very reason for our existence.

In a previously quoted passage from James Jordan's *The Musician's Soul*, one of my favorite phrases is his description of Center as that place from which "one's being holds forth." Indeed, the very juxtaposition of the words "holds" and "forth" is interesting in that while "holding" suggests staying put, "forth" suggests movement forward. Is it possible for both efforts to co-exist? It is not only possible, but necessary, at least for the quality of journey toward Center to which this book is devoted. This very balance/counterbalance, this yin/yang, is one of the most important concepts this book offers—it is certainly a concept that captures my imagination.

As artists, storytellers of one walk or another, we have a responsibility to communicate and share. Center is not merely a place to sit or stay, but rather a place *from which* we give and express—a launching pad for *doing*. The goal is to remain connected—no matter how far-reaching the gestures of giving and expressing may be. And in those moments when we do find ourselves disconnected, the challenge then becomes about how to get back—how to reconnect.

Note:
The simple solid,
filled circle or sphere is one
of the oldest symbols representing
"the center" and is most common in
rock carvings. Having no beginning or
end, it can symbolize the universe,
eternity or wholeness.

The Role of Breath and Center

As a teaching artist attempting to define and impart a process for performing, I find myself hearkening, time and time again, to the life-defining gesture of breath. It has become the method, as well as the metaphor, for almost everything I teach—even the title assigned to this chapter has its relationship to breath. The journey inward might well be described as (it certainly has the opportunity to be accomplished by) the inhalation, while the outward expression might be associated with the exhalation. And one might even describe art, or life, as everything that happens "along the way."

Breathing is a miraculous and enormously complex action. This particular perusal will be general and simple; but hopefully—through those very generalities and simplifications—substantive and illuminating as a method for travel towards, and from, Center.

The Many Facets of Breath

Breath is comprised of two functions: inhalation and exhalation. It is the responsibility of inhalation (at least in singing and acting) to open, oxygenate, and exhilarate the instrument…it is *precedent*, and it is required. It is also at this very point of inhalation that we are offered that all-important moment for "visiting" the idea that occasions expression and/or action…the reason for speaking, singing, or moving. Inhalation is figuratively, as well as literally, our inspiration.

On the other hand, it is the *opportunity* of exhalation to express—to share and communicate—all that was "visited" during inhalation. The challenge for exhalation is that it begins (or, in truth, *continues* the cycle begun by inhalation) as soon as inhalation has completed its own task—without those inhibitors known as judgment or editing. The great tenor, Luciano Pavarotti, has been credited with saying that sound should actually begin during the last second of inhalation—that waiting or delaying is an opportunity for "constriction." And constriction is arguably the number one enemy of the instrument. When expression (or exhalation) is delayed, then that which we are called upon to express often becomes edited…sometimes even withheld.

We can all agree that remaining connected is key. Don Greene's terms, "centering down" and "centering up," imply a *connection* to place—a specific place we are trying to go to and from. James Jordan's fascination with the symbolism of the circle (enso) and the perpetual motion it epitomizes, is the perfect mapping for inspiration/inhalation and expression/exhalation. The desire for breath to be cyclic (expressed earlier) is perhaps better expressed as the desire to avoid interruption, or break, in the *flow*. If it is the nature of breath to connect us, then what happens at those inevitable points of disconnect…how do we get back? How do we sustain the connection?

We have discussed sustaining the cycle of breath, avoiding those "hesitancies" that rob expression. From a broader perspective, we can apply the nature of sustaining to the actor's thought or objective, the singer's sound or phrase, the dancer's physical action, and the teacher's intention. And we need to undo a misconception. "Support," the word most often used to describe the action associated with sustaining, is one of the most misquoted and misunderstood concepts in our lexicon of technical terminology. The Oxford English Dictionary online (www.oed.com) defines *support* as: "to keep something going over time or continuously." Support, more often than not, becomes a rigid and locked-down version of *holding on*, rather than a supple way of continuing action. Inherent in the Oxford English Dictionary definition is its nod to *instruction*—hopefully, enough said. But when support falters and connection fails, then what? My students have heard me say, more often than they would care to hear, that "redemption is but one inhale away." The challenge is to avoid the distraction of disconnection until the new inhale can occur. Honestly, it's as simple as that: trusting, knowing, that the circle awaits us.

So, inhalation inspires, exhalation expresses, and both of these actions function as part of a cycle/circle that should never be halted or interrupted by any physical and/or mental hesitancies. We (mind, body, and spirit) are the terrain, the vessel; breath is the vehicle; and Center is that place within us where we travel to and communicate from. It is a "supple" home-place from which beings *do*…that place, indeed, from which "one's being holds forth."

Six

Stanislavsky's Circles of Attention

Nova Thomas

An artist must have full use of his own spiritual, human material because that is the only stuff from which he can fashion a living soul for his part.

In my involvement with the new methods of inner technique, I sincerely believed that to express the **experience** [i.e., what the character goes through in the course of the play], the actor need only master the creative state, and all the rest will follow.

The essence of art is not in its external forms, but in its spiritual content. (p. 47)

—Bella Merlin
The Complete Stanislavsky Toolkit

Konstantin Stanislavsky, the great Russian actor, director, and theorist, remains, arguably, the most significant figure in the history of actor training. Spirituality was at the very core of his renowned "system." Stanislavsky was fascinated by many aspects and teachings of yoga, particularly the concept of *prana*, or energy…life force (even though the term was never used because Stanislavsky was writing in Soviet Russia during a time when such spiritual studies were repressed). As Sharon Carnicke explains in *Stanislavsky in Focus*:

he (Stanislavsky) used *prana* to ground his analysis of communication in the theater. Rays of energy between actors and their partners, as well as actors and their audiences, become "the vehicle for infecting the spectator with the artist's emotion." This concept of shared energy informed important exercises in communication, and at the origin of those great teachings was another important tool for the actor: the "concentration of attention." (p. 141)

During performance, Stanislavsky expects actors to give their full spiritual, mental, and physical attention (in other words, their total concentration) to the actions of the stage, their scene partners, and the objects necessary to their work. He calls all these points of focus, whether animate or inanimate, the "objects" of attention. Successful concentration fosters a state of mind that appears to isolate actors from anything external to the world of the play, what he calls "public solitude." He trains actors to concentrate by defining "circles of attention," and actors learn to control and limit their focus. (p. 171)

Note:

Ancient symbol

found in petroglyphics. Used

in alchemy this symbol has meant

"essence," "spirit," or to "distill." In

modern times it can connotate

"focus," or as one may interpret, the

distillation or essence

of an action.

This desire for, and ability to, *focus* is an obsession with all artists (with anyone, in all honesty, wanting to achieve success at a given task). In a world that is riddled with noise and distraction—for our specific purposes, in performing situations where left-brain judgments, self-doubts, and distractions can contaminate any artistic moment—concentration and focus are key.

Concentration, at least as it is most often perceived, is too limiting if we merely "journey inward," sit down, and isolate ourselves from the artist's first responsibility: expression. Jon Kabat-Zinn in his national bestseller, *Wherever You Go There You Are*, wrote: "concentration practice…by itself resembles a state of withdrawal from the world. Its characteristic energy is closed, rather than open, absorbed rather than available, trancelike rather than fully awake…it can be of great value, but it can also be seriously limiting if…you come to see it as a refuge from life." (p. 74)

The Circles of Attention

Nova Thomas

An enormously valuable counter-consideration to the more common practices of concentrating and focusing may be found in this Stanislavskian idea of "circles of attention." These defined ways and means and "spaces" can be a great aid to concentration and focus: by defining and limiting an area of focus, concentration is not quite such an overwhelming task. Stanislavsky's discussions and teachings are dedicated to an actor's work, and are specifically defined in many of the texts dedicated to his System, but for the purposes of our work, these circles have been redefined for the lyric-actor and teacher of singers and actors.

As performers we need to *position* ourselves *in relationship to* our feelings, ideas, concepts, given circumstances, objectives, needs, other people, and/ or objects in the scene. *Positioning* requires an understanding of who we are in any given circumstance, whether a musician responsible to someone else's idea, an actor responsible to another character and that character's story, a dancer responsible to the possibilities of physical expression, or a teacher responsible for bringing others along in the process of learning. Once we understand who we are and what our basic duties are to self/character (the task at hand, or objective), then we have the opportunity and responsibility to consider our relationship to all things "other." These Stanislavskian circles of attention bring specificity and order to the expression of these relationships. They are extended expressions—concentric circles—of awareness.

The first circle is the most intimate one. It is the one that relates to innermost feeling, want, or desire. It relates to those things (ideas or objects) that are closest to us…the smallest object or point. It is the area that encompasses the performer's immediate body, mind, and spirit. It could also be an object on one's person or in one's grasp.

The second circle is the circle that includes others. It includes the person or persons you're *directly* talking to. It is the *immediate* area around us. It could also include an object of attention… something that one directly and specifically notices.

The third circle is the largest and most inclusive. It can include God, the world, a large space, the landscape, the entire audience, the entire chorus or orchestra, or the biggest/grandest version of an idea, desire, or expression. The area of focus is large and encompassing.

Note:

Caduceus, the snake-entwined staff of Hermes, messenger of the gods. Ancient symbol of communication and trade also can denote a marketing place. Notice the three circles, touching, yet the last circle is open, almost like an invitation.

In looking at the performance of a script or score, the first circle might be the most intimate (personal) idea: the monologue, the most personally reflective music, or the softest expression. The second circle deals with the person or persons you're speaking directly to: it's the duet, trio or other small ensemble; the small scene; the counterpoint to an original idea; the immediate obstacle; an object that captures your attention; or the dialogue. The third circle is that largest point of view and perspective: it might be a ranting at the Almighty, an expression of the largest desire of one's heart, an expression of that which is *super*-natural, an observation of those aspects of life that are larger than (or at least as large as) life, a declaration, a pronouncement, an orchestra at full tilt, a choir at *fortissimo*, a soloist or character in a climactic moment, or the scene or moment that expresses the most heightened dramatic circumstances.

The advantages of knowing in any given moment "where one is," as well as the space one is responsible for occupying, are clear. We are often caught either "pushing" an idea or expression at the audience, randomly spewing (and therefore, wasting) energy, being entirely too small or closed, or just looking lost. The circles give us a *specific* place to be, a quantifiable space to fill, and even a parameter on which to focus our attention.

Translation: The Circles of Attention

James Jordan

Based upon Stanislavsky's ideas above, it might be helpful to think of these circles in yet another way. The circles of attention might be defined in contemporaneous terms as three distinctive levels of attention that can be exercised by any performing artist. While any performance experience is dependent on all three circles occurring to maintain pedagogical balance within the rehearsal or performance process, an artist must be aware that (1) the three circles exist at all and (2) an artful and artistic rehearsal process is dependent upon how supply the artist can move between the circles.

The challenge of developing this aspect of artistic technique is to be able to move between these three circles as warranted by the dynamic of the musical situation. Many persons I observe live almost exclusively in the second circle.

First Circle: The Personal/Spiritual Circle

This is the most inward and central circle of awareness. This circle is highly personal and contains the stuff of who we are. The quality of being in this circle is very contemplative and even silent. It is in this circle we all should be just prior to the start of any piece of music. This circle is most efficiently entered through the breath.

Second Circle: The Relational Circle

It is at this level that much of the stuff of rehearsals, and later performance, is accomplished. One's energies, both physical and listening, are directed outward when occupying this circle: toward specific sections of the ensemble and all sections when performing together. The energy of this circle is distinctly different from the energy of the first circle, and its energy moves outward towards the ensemble.

Third Circle: The Ideas and Interpretative Circle

This is the circle where interpretive ideas and inspiration of sounds and texts live and, in fact, are born. Many of us in the musicing process live in this circle almost exclusively. It is in this circle where we may be most vulnerable to excessive verbalism. Some verbalism may be necessary within this circle, but excessive verbalism runs the risk of detaching us from the connection with the sound itself or the artistic creation. This circle relies heavily on the ability to listen. A caution also must be extended to not use this circle when elements of the first and second circles would better serve the greater process. Within this circle live the spiritual and life messages of any piece of music. This is also the circle in which honesty of sound, word, movement, and music in general is nurtured and nourished.

The Travel and Transfer Medium between the Circles: Listening

One can never underestimate the power of the listening ear to any performing artist. By nature, human beings want to be listened to. In fact, listening to others in daily life is how human connections are created, forged, and strengthened. In music, connections between and among artists can only be likewise created, forged, and strengthened if a high level of aware listening is activated and engaged. This engagement of the ear is established not only because of an intense desire on the part of the artist to listen, but also because of a passion to listen and hear others and what *their* voices have to say. Other than the breath, there is perhaps no more powerful tool than listening for any artist. Listening informs, connects, personalizes, profoundly humanizes, and deepens every rehearsal experience. Listening also lives in the wordless world of the creative and fully alive artist, for it is a language all its own, specialized through the sounds of music and actualized through sung word or body motion.

Now if we step back and examine this entire paradigm, we can begin to understand the innermost psychology of the artist's psyche. We move with ease and comfort between the three levels and, most importantly, are aware at all times where we are operating. We must also monitor when one or more of the circles are being ignored in the rehearsal process. In rehearsal and performance, listening to oneself is as important as listening to the others, and we must effortlessly move between these two intense ways of listening.

Rehearsals and performances must be constant journeys inward and outward between these circles. However, it must be noted that when performing, we begin a performance in the first circle, but once the sound is birthed, the final rehearsed creative act lives intensely in the third circle.

To be an efficient rehearsal technician, we need to have some awareness of a psychological process, or at the very least a bias rooted in some paradigm on what actually goes on within both rehearsal and performance. Such a paradigm moves the rehearsal and performance from a murky progression of events into a realm where rehearsal and performance events are connected to each other with meaning. Just as we learn the art of singing or playing an instrument, and yes, even performing, that journey is always marked by an understanding of not only the process, but also the path that the process can and should take. Awareness of these three circles is your admission to a better, more profound and life-affirming, and ultimately humane, process for artistic creation.

Seven

Humility Is the Core of Center

James Jordan

This is why, in an act of imitation, every afternoon that I am at home finds me in my backyard for fifteen minutes tending to what has become the fourth component of my daily spiritual practice. For as long as I can remember that practice begins, on arising, with hatha yoga for the body, a reading from a religious classic for my mind, and a blend of prayer and meditation for my spirit. Those three practices remain in place, but it helps to have them grounded, and that is what the addition of composting accomplishes. Being physically anchored to the earth helps us to keep my ego from bobbing along mindlessly on the sea of life. (p. 210)

—Huston Smith
The Way Things Are

It came to me that the soul is like a castle made exclusively of diamond or some other very clear crystal. In this castle are a multitude of dwellings, just as in heavens there are many mansions.
(p. 35)

—Saint Teresa of Avila
The Interior Castle

Art is not a pastime but a priesthood. (p. 119)

—Jean Cocteau

Walking in This World by Julia Cameron

Always wish that you may find patience enough in yourself to endure, and simplicity enough to believe; that you may acquire more and more confidence in that which is difficult, and in your solitude among others. (p. 120)

—Rainer Maria Rilke

Walking in This World by Julia Cameron

Humility can be both a curse and a blessing, and the same can be said for ego, too. Flexibility or firmness, gentle concern or ruthless determination, collaboration or competition: which is more important, which will contribute to our music making? Do we even have a choice?...

Egotistical behavior can alienate, antagonize, and polarize those around you, isolate you, and even help you to lose your job; and yet every artist I have interviewed feels that a healthy ego is essential to artistry. The question remains: how do we strike a healthy balance between humility and ego? (p. 225)

When you use ego to compete against another person rather than striving within yourself, the game changes from an Inner Game of artistry to an Outer Game of "beat the competition"—and that's not a game you can ever really win, because it zaps your energy, it takes attention away from the music. (p. 234)

—Barry Green

The Mastery of Music

I am not sure
I have explained this
well. Self-knowledge is so
important that I do not care
how high you are raised up to
the heavens. I never want you
to cease cultivating it. As long as
we are on this earth, there is nothing
more essential than humility. Enter the
room of self-knowledge first, instead
of floating to other places. This is
the path. Traveling along a safe and
level road, who needs wings to fly?
Let's make the best possible use
of our feet first and learn
to know ourselves.
(p. 46)

Do you think
that your deep
humility, your
self-sacrifice, your
bountiful charity and
commitment to being
of service to all beings
meaningless? (p. 294)

—Saint Teresa of Avila
The Interior Castle

As I recently
meditated on the term *mudra*,
I became particularly aware of the symbol of
a lock. A lock always conceals a secret. We frequently
use gestures in an unconscious way to seal something;
for example, when giving special weight to a decision, or reaching
an agreement with another person, or even with cosmic
consciousness. In precisely the same way, we may also seal something
with our inner forces—we reach an understanding with ourselves.
(p. 3) The outer circumstances of our lives usually shape themselves
according to our imagination and the contents of our minds.
So we have the possibility of shaping our inner images in such
a way that we enjoy life, experience success in our work,
and have relationships on a loving and understanding
basis. It is very important to create an unshakable
faith and be filled with both fervor and
serenity to accompany
our self-made images.
We need to create little
experiences of success for
ourselves, since what functions
in a small way will also succeed
on an larger scale. (pp. 14–15)

—Gertrud Hirschi
Mudras: Yoga in Your Hands

If we ponder what feelings are operating when bad or insensitive things happen in artists and where those feelings live, we can certainly attest that at those moments, there is a total absence of humility. Humility is directly related to our individual importance to both the world and to music—humility concerning the respect and admiration for the gifts and opinions of others—humility concerning the value of every human being.

Artists who assert their egos upon others or on an ensemble are at that moment in a state of unawareness about their simple little place in the world. The only music that matters is what "they" make. Often they are so self-absorbed that they never hear the music that is a product of their somewhat distorted self-portrayal. Many great artists that I know and have known come with humility always intact and operating. No matter what the circumstance, no matter the quality of the music they are either rehearsing or performing, they are at all times humble. Their humbleness seems to magnify the good in people and the good sounds around them.

If humility as a natural default is not innate in our being, the good news is that it can be both learned and practiced. The following story touched me deeply and further convinced me that the daily practice of humility is an important factor in creating a Center within each of us.

Note:

Pueblo kiva design.

An underground chamber used for important spiritual ceremonies and social gatherings.

Trash Is "Refreshing"

"I have a need to replenish myself, especially emotionally," says Noble, who claims that gathering debris is his R and R. "I do a lot of traveling and teaching and rehearsing and expend a lot of emotional energy. Picking up trash is totally physical so it is bound to be refreshing."

And educational, too, he's quick to add. Noble's garbage expeditions on one college site where fires had destroyed buildings in 1889 and 1942 led him to some stunning speculations on man's relationship with trash, from past to present.

"I was amazed by the amount of Noxzema used and you must remember that this was a men's dorm," he says, shaking his head in bewilderment. "I don't really know what that means."

He says today, that plastic is the most prevalent form of refuse, that fewer and fewer cigarette packages are found, and that he can tell when students are approaching mid-terms or finals from all the broken glass around.

"I haven't made a scientific study, but during the pressure points of the college year you are more apt to find broken glass," he explains. "I think you can see how that is a result of student frustration."

No theories are available why the false teeth wound up under some trees. Or how the stop sign made its way to the bottom of a ravine. Or the reasons behind all those watches, keys, hunting boots, shoes and socks, letters (he never reads them) and money that Noble has hauled off in his rounds, which often begin at dawn.

"I sometimes wonder what the campus janitors think when they see those trash cans full of all this unusual stuff," says Noble.

It was estimated that he has put in 210 hours in his clean-up campaign that has covered half the hills surrounding the campus, the football stadium, a city park and sidewalks to and from his home. After beginning his treks with only a small shopping bag, he has now graduated to carrying large cans he gets from the school cafeteria.

"I guess this has always been part of my nature," says Noble, who admits that only lately did he realize that there was a janitor inside him just dying to get out. "This is my form of jogging and there is such a wonderful sense of accomplishment. The time goes so fast. One would wonder what would occupy the mind at this time, but you are really absorbed in it. I guess it's just that you're always looking for something."

In a way, that's comforting to Noble. He does not deny that, maybe someday, this could lead to a whole new career.

"I know that I could be happy as a custodian," he says. "It's that element of service, making people happy. Ever since the seventh grade one of my life's desires has to become a waiter."

Noble's family might not be nearly so surprised to learn of his janitorial ambitions.

After all, he was the only one who never had to be told to clean his room.

—Wilfred F. Bunge
Warmly, Weston: A Luther College Life, pp. 134–135

According to Wilfred Bunge, Weston Noble attributes his persistent litter collection to his personality. Noble wishes at times that he were not so compulsive. I, however, have another theory, perhaps a theory that resonates in the souls of all great artists.

When I first heard this story, I was a bit shocked and very taken aback. Here was a conductor whom I hold in the highest regard, and his major pastime is picking up trash! I couldn't believe it. This quiet, gentle soul who makes such beautiful and honest music, spends the beginning of his days gathering campus debris.

My first thought was "this is a bit abnormal." But then I read this and began to understand why we might all consider engaging in such an activity. Musicians as a group have an almost inherited tendency to elevate themselves in their own minds as being "better" than others, and when it is necessary, they forcefully impose themselves upon others. The justifications are almost always "for the music." Humility and humbleness are nowhere to be found, just omnipresent ego and oppressive energies, which tend to stifle the spirits of all those around. Such persons create no circumstances in which to practice some form of personal humility.

Imagine. Weston Noble, one of this century's greatest choral conductors and human beings, does not think too highly of himself to pick up trash. How many "great artists" do you know who would do this, or anything that even resembles this? One of the reasons Noble has done this for years is that, for some reason, *service* coupled with a certain kind of *humbleness* brings incredible peace and calm to his soul and to his daily routine. In this he practices a form of humility every day. I recently saw a beautiful photographic essay of the Trappist Monks in Spencer, Massachusetts. Images of the cloakroom for their work clothes show that their garb for their workday—working in the fields at seemingly "mundane" tasks—serves to both ground them and invest them in a type of humbleness that only working with their hands can impart.

Perhaps a reason why artists lack human skills of humility, compassion, and love as they make music is that they do not engage in any activity that places them in a true service and serving capacity. Gardening, planting, cleaning streets, picking up trash, or volunteering to work in a food kitchen might all serve to keep us in touch with our innate and humble "core."

Truly great artists have a remarkable humility about what they do. They believe that they possess no unique gifts other than a love and passion for making music. Humbleness is a daily part of their lives in some way, and that presence of humbleness carries over into their music and their way of relating to others. But more importantly, it is this sense of "humbleness" that creates a place within us for Center to occupy, and perhaps grow.

I was thinking about teachers of mine who used humbleness as the medium of instruction. Actually, I came up with many, but one stands out.

Sarah Farley was my third grade teacher (of whom I spoke earlier in this book). What I realized is that this very early experience in my life did much to establish my centering place. It seems clear now that in order for us to have Center, that "place" of Center must be established, or perhaps created, not by one but by a series of life-shaping, opening experiences. Center is a place deep within that is first created and then maintained through many experiences, which inhabit the same place. Centering experiences are those that make us aware of the world and people around us, and they point out to us, in a gentle, loving way, that we are not alone in this world.

A stocky and gruff woman, Sarah Farley was one of my favorite teachers. She was very good at teaching third grade things. But every day of class, she talked to us, tiny third graders, about sharing—sharing our *selves* and possessions with others. Sharing of all types received lavish praise in that room. In fact, the entire school year was a study in sharing with others. Imagine a course in humility through sharing at that very impressionable age. To this day, I remember how good it felt to give away something we created, how good it was to share lunch with someone in the class who had less, and how good it was to do without so that others could have. We "cleaned" every day! She explained that it was noble to be in service to others. I vividly recall how beautiful I felt every day of that year, that none of us fought with each other and that we all perceived each other as equals. In that class we never had individual projects; we always participated in group projects, which taught us that we were all equal. That year was an incredible experience in humility in service to others other than ourselves.

Some of the greatest artists have existed at the poverty level while they made great art. The stories of the destitute and humble existence of Béla Bartók are legendary. Mother Teresa lived with only bare essentials in her life of service to a higher good. Many great musicians grew up in humble circumstances in the beginnings of their lives. My father was a self-employed auto mechanic. Every day I watched him labor in dirt and grease to repair cars and make a living. He never complained or wanted for something better in his life. An orphan, I am certain that my father knew humility. Manual labor was a noble task. It was his way of serving. He was always thankful to be able to make a living in that way. And through his garage, he not only repaired cars, but he performed countless acts of kindness, which I witnessed. He was a man who taught me Center by being centered.

This story about Weston Noble prompted me to ponder the connection between working with our hands and the intimacy of humility and humbleness. Hands have a unique way of connecting us to our humble core. In fact, many believe it is through the hands that one maintains contact with the elemental world. In hatha yoga, there are twenty-five *mudras*—that is, hand, body, and eye positions. In a book entitled *Mudras: Yoga in Your Hands,* Gertrud Hirschi writes that through a practice of "hand yoga" we can gain understanding of our oneness and humanity within a larger world—a type of humility? When we gain an understanding of our inner forces, we gain an understanding of both ourselves and others.

So at the core of Weston Noble's trash gathering is much more than an eccentric habit. It is his personal type of yoga mudra. It is working with his hands. It is a daily yearning to work with his hands that provides insight to himself. Picking up trash calms him and gives him solace. It is through that trash collection that his soul refreshes its humility daily. Each day that humility plays a pivotal role in his teaching and music making. Part of a musician's "walk" should, perhaps, be a daily and planned task that keeps us grounded and humble.

Back to Story

Perhaps Center is created and formed within us from without, first. Experiences cause us to know our Center, and we tend to anchor those experiences deep within. But we must also have the ability to recognize those experiences as being formative to a piece of our Center. Our story plays a powerful role in our lives as people, and certainly as musicians. However, it is our ability to recall our life stories that deepens a part of our Center. Recalling those experiences that made us "feel" for the first time can only serve to energize our center so that particular Center is perceivable to others. If we believe in Center, then we must also realize that our Center exists. That spiritual place is first hollowed out within us by life and life alone. Life, and perhaps the humbleness of life, not only defines our Center but also the sheer size and power of it.

Note:
"ADINKRAHENE"
West African Adinkra cloth symbol
meaning charisma, greatness
and leadership.

Eight

Center: A Way of Being and Living

James Jordan

I love the recklessness of faith. First you leap, and then you grow wings. (p. 7)

—William Sloane Coffin
Credo

The central images in this book are taken from the potter's craft: centering, and ordeal by fire. But both are archetypal and occur in other contexts as well. Centering is a term used by Quakers for a feeling of flowing toward a common center in their meetings for worship. It is also an ancient Sanskrit term used in spiritual disciplines of the East. What it means, I think, is to feel the whole in every part. When you center clay on a potter's wheel, you take a lump of clay, and by moving it upwards in a cone and outwards in a plane, you create a condition of balance between the outside and the inside, so that when you touch the clay at a single point, the whole mass is affected. Centering has nothing to do with a center as a place. (p. 55)

Centering is a discipline of surrendering in this sense of receptivity, and of integrating. Moving in from the outside toward a center which is not a space, but a function, a balance, a feature; distributing the center itself from within outwards. By undergoing a change on the inside, the clay comes as we say into center: which is a quality, not a place. (p. 56)

The inner path seems to have this self-renewing, self-correcting, self-completing quality. What the psychologist Jung called "the creative purposeful." As we walk the path, we make careful observations and testings, mapping the territory, and this becomes our silence. The science of any period is the map of its reality. It lies always between the last insight and the next.

A science of the whole man is undivisive, and takes in all the evidence of man as a being of body, soul, and spirit, who not only has eyes and ears but is a see-er and a hearer, and whose experiences through the body bespeak another realm. (p. 179)

—Mary Caroline Richards
The Crossing Point

The classic Buddhist metaphor for the ordinary state of our minds is a monkey jumping here and there, constantly distracted, restless, and on the move. The monkey mind always races on to the next thing before fully experiencing what's happening right now. Her speedy mind continually closes the gap, filling it with a random scattering of half-thoughts, memories, reveries, daydreams— anything at all. (p. 329)

—Tara Bennett-Goleman
Emotional Alchemy

Probably the first and most important "thing" I ever learned about the art of conducting revolved around the word "Center." For several months in my first year in graduate school, my private lessons with Elaine Brown all revolved around her wanting to impart to me the meaning and importance of Center. I remember thinking at the time that this seemed to be a long time spent on something I thought I understood! Well, I can assure you that Dr. Brown's fastidiousness about "making" me understand Center was the single most important thing that I learned from her, or anyone for that matter. In retrospect, Center is in all that I do, and that knowledge of Center as imparted by Elaine and others since then has transformed me. Without Center, without working off of a "central core," musical sounds will never communicate. For singers without Center, their sound lacks both resonance and communicative power. In dancers, movement seems to be, at best, peripheral motion.

First it was a thing I sensed but could not describe. There was a "strength" in what Dr. Brown did, but I really couldn't put my finger on it. It was an energy from her to me (us) that was powerful, direct, and *immediate*. After a period of time, I remember becoming subtly aware of when Center was present or absent in the room. Initially it was all intimately related to the musical sound; however, I was not aware that the presence of Center was what made the sound different. Sung sounds without being centered seemed to have a "gauzy" quality and lacked rhythmic vitality.

It is now clear that this "thing" we call "Center" is present within great musicians and all inspired performances. Its absence or presence makes the difference between pedantic musicing and inspired, life-changing musicing. Centeredness in teaching transforms a mundane classroom into a living and vital experience. My first real experience of Center, outside my work with Elaine Brown, was my first encounter with Carlo Maria Giulini, the great

Italian conductor, and the Verdi Requiem. Giulini was a man who personified Center in every conducting gesture. Every gesture had profound meaning because it came out of *his* Center.

The Locus of Center

In the first lessons with Dr. Brown, she attempted to bring me to an understanding of my own physical center. She would always say that center was "a quality, not a place." She also told me that "center" is the name given to a "serendipitous" coincidence of important "human" events.

Dr. Brown described physical Center as an implanted gyroscope. When in

place, no matter how I moved as a conductor, my gesture would have meaning because then, according to her, all gesture is an outgrowth of Center. Center has the effect of a counterbalance; it roots us to the earth but is also the spiritual energy core where we live.

And then she began the first of many discussions on Martin Buber, *I and Thou*. According to Brown (and Buber), there can be no real meaningful communication between human beings without Center connecting to Center. Center knows no gender, no bias—it is unfettered, direct communication, one to one. And according to Brown (and Buber), it is the most powerful of stuff.

Elaine Brown's close association with John Finley Williamson and Westminster Choir College is most likely the source of her inspiration and interest in Center. Williamson was a man of great personal charisma. His gift was an ability to understand and foster spiritual connection in his singers. While he believed that "tone" was the hallmark of what he did, those who sang for Dr. Williamson all remember his remarkable and compelling human presence. The germ of this idea is demonstrated in the following quote:

> It is a mistake to believe that in our conducting we must have points to our beats so that the choir can keep time. Singers do not keep time because of what they see. They keep time because of the forward-moving rhythmic pace the conductor creates through empathy. When one sings under a great master he cannot make a mistake because he is too busy to stop and think. The conductor presses him forward with such electrifying power that he hasn't time to think how many beats he gives to a note or even what pitch he is singing. Everything in sound moves forward with such urgency that it is impossible to do anything other than the right thing. (p. 198)

—John Finley Williamson

John Finley Williamson (1887–1964): His Life and Contribution to Choral Music by David A. Wehr

Center exists unmistakably within us. Its absence creates a type of emptiness in any performance or rehearsal space and creates a cloud in the communicative atmosphere in which musicians thrive. Center must be recognized, fostered, and nurtured, and in a way, this process is the most important thing an artist can do to "be" as he or she really is in front of others. Center is a great gift to others. Because of its inherent power, Center provides wordless stability to all who come in contact with it. The power of Center is infectious and, perhaps, is at the core of the definition of what it is to be fully alive as a musician/artist in the world.

Nine

BEING and TOGETHER

Nova Thomas

The performing arts are most often an ensemble effort. *Centering* and *being* are most often associated with *individual* efforts—solo journeys. Is it possible then, or even necessary, for a *group* of individuals to have a single, *additional* center—a *plural* being? When brought together, do individually found centers and states of being automatically create a centered entity? Or is there another opportunity with—another responsibility to—a *collective* effort?

James Jordan is one of the most influential choral conductors in America; his ensembles are renowned…loved. He can speak to (and has) the art and alchemy of ensemble building far better than I. But I would like to share a few of my own experiences and observances with the plural pronouns—on the stage, as well as in the classroom.

As performers, we do much of our preparation and technical work alone. Practice rooms, those usually dingy forums for the building and habituation of necessary skills sets, are cubicles "for one." We rarely have opportunities, or the need, to practice together. Yet our performances (including the precedent rehearsals) are almost always collaborative—a group effort. As a performer, the rehearsal space—that exciting forum in which individual talents, minds, personalities, and spirits collide—is always an eagerly awaited joy. As a teacher, my awe expands daily in the presence of the power of the collective in a classroom. And sometimes it's magic…other times, not. This I know: When great artists or eager students come together, there is a possibility for the miraculous; and when individual greatness is illusive, there is that possibility, in numbers, for rescue. There is indeed a separate and additional energy in the collective. The challenge is to identify and create that "thing," perhaps a *Center* or *state of being*, that includes us all, and yet is held hostage by no one—a place and existence that gathers and focuses individual lives and gifts to the service of something larger.

Most successful endeavors begin with a collective task. For singers, it is the first sing-through; for actors, the first read-through. At that time, it is wonderful to simply witness your own character in the company of others. This generally puts everyone on the same *page*, but it doesn't necessarily put everyone in the same *place*.

Having had the privilege of working with great directors and conductors, and having been a student of great classroom teachers, it is interesting now as a teacher myself to try to identify exactly what it was that these masters and mentors did to create that greater whole. One of the things that seems to be consistent is the identification and agreement of what any story or endeavor is truly about. Once a theme is defined and agreed upon, we have the opportunity to see ourselves in something larger than our own set of circumstances—the *world* of the play (or the music, or the dance, or the classroom) gets bigger. Another commonality is the identification of an ensuing objective, or that one overriding thing that the story hopes to accomplish by being told at all—the *reason* for the play (or the music, or the dance, or the classroom) gets bigger. These two efforts bring individuals into a collective *service*…and I've never seen that do anything but bear fruit. A third effort that is perhaps not as profound as the last two, but nonetheless resonant, belongs to the exercise of *playing together*. Under relaxed and less serious circumstances, we tend to discover commonalities…and those commonalities can illuminate shared places…and those shared places are powerful launching pads for creating together. These endeavors, as well as many others not mentioned, help us as a group to go somewhere…to find a collective Center…and from that collective Center, to *be*, and ultimately *do*, something that we could not be or do alone.

At the beginning of every semester in every class, I set about the tasks my own masters and mentors put before me. We identify the *theme*, define the *objectives*, establish in mind the potential our accomplishments might have for *service*, and move on to exercises that simply put us all in the room together (in some cases, playing together). The exercise that we regularly return to is the most primal and fundamental of all efforts—*breath*.

Organizing ourselves in pairs, we simply inhale and exhale, usually to counts of four, together. After inhaling and exhaling simultaneously, we then move to a sort of "exchange" of breath—one person inhales while the other exhales. (This aspect of the exercise is also expressed with physical movement where, in coordination with the inhaling and exhaling, we lean toward and away from one another.) Pairs become quartets, quartets become octets, and eventually the entire class comes together in one big circle where, through a rhythmic process of inhaling and exhaling, the individuals give to, and take from, the center of the circle. We discover, in this cyclic rhythm of exchange, the art of giving and receiving, together. A cohort of individuals are existing and radiating from this great Center defined by the most fundamental expression of any state of being—breath. And the results are palpable.

Bella Merlin, in her book, *The Complete Stanislavsky Toolkit,* describes Stanislavsky's own journey and challenges he faced bringing performers together. His language is specific to the director and defines three key principles a director must tackle:

How to work with the author

How to work with the actors

How to work with everyone else involved in the production

(p. 180)

It is easy to see that these principles might also define *states of being* that a group of individuals must prioritize:

How to be with the original intent of the author, composer,
or choreographer

How to be with the other actors, singers, dancers, or students

How to be with everyone else involved in the effort

Being must then become *doing.* But that's another chapter…

Ten

The Space Within: Lowering Your Physical Center

James Jordan

We dance round in a ring and suppose,
but the Secret sits in the middle and knows. (p. 133)

—Robert Frost
Enso by Audrey Yoshiko Seo

Zen teachers like to draw circles. Sometimes they draw them around from right to left, sometimes around from left to right. These circles can represent emptiness, fullness, or the moon. Or they can represent practice. The circle that goes around from right to left—against the path of the sun on the sundial—represents the hard way of practice before any glimmer of understanding appears. When it goes around from left to right, following the path of the sun, it represents the easier way of practice after a glimmer opens the Way. But both before and after the glimmer, the practice requires investment and conscientious diligence. (p. 82)

—Robert Aitken
The Morning Star: New and Selected Zen Writings

I believe in man's unconscious, the deep spring from which comes his power to communicate and to love. For me, all art is a combination of these powers; art is nothing to me if it does not make contact between the creator and the perceiver on an unconscious level. Let us say that love is the way we have of communicating personally in the deepest way. What art can do is to extend this communication, magnify it, and carry it to vastly greater numbers of people. In this it needs a warm core, a hidden heating element. Without that core, art is only an exercise in techniques, a calling of attention to the artist, or a vain display. I believe in art for the warmth and love it carries within it, even if it be the lightest entertainment, or the bitterest satire, or the most shattering tragedy. For if art is cold it cannot communicate anything to anybody. (pp. 141–142)

—Leonard Bernstein
Findings

The problem with Center is that it is composed of almost equal parts conceptual and physical. And in actuality, the spiritual is a bit easier to get at than the physical. Yet without a clearly felt and *perceived* physical Center, any human message, let alone artistic message, will be transmitted as a blur, a series of muted energies, which have little or no impact on those at the recieving end of the communication experience. Center clarifies and crystallizes human and musical messages to listeners.

A teacher of conducting I once observed had only one strong and vocal admonition: "Go deeper." While that phrase certainly summarizes the problem succinctly, it provides little or no information on how to travel to that place. And going deeper actually hides the real issues. While one must go deeper within oneself philosophically, that depth of connection will never be found if a physical space is not prepared or understood.

After years of working with musicians and conductors, and revisiting my lessons with Elaine Brown, the issue is not feeling some type of Center, but feeling it low enough within the body to make a profound difference on the art we attempt to influence and create. Center, when grounded within us, feels very low and deeply inward while at the same time incredibly spacious. Achieving this depth of Center has to do with locating an intimate *kinesthetic* understanding of physical self, and then placing one's spiritual "contents" into that place within the body. The great Irish poet William Butler Yeats has perhaps the best description: he calls that place "the deep heart's core,"[6] and that phrase is perhaps the best explanation of what I will now attempt to describe. The remarkable thing about this Center is that it can migrate within the body, almost having a will of its own. It can exist high in the body, low in the body, or not exist at all! Some musicians attempt to carry on with their art without any awareness of their own Center. Center must be willed spiritually *and* kinesthetically to its deepest location when we desire to communicate anything to anyone. Center must be in place and anchored in its location first before all else. Breath will never come into the body and energy will never flow outward unless one *both* wills and anchors one's Center within the body.

Willing Center

My first three months of private conducting study were spent studying Center. That study was a combination of reading and physical activities, and finally, how all gesture, performing and musicing emanates from that core. The two books that made me understand, at least in a cognitive way, the idea of Center were *Centering in Poetry, Pottery and the Person* by Mary Caroline

---

6   This phrase can be found at the end of what is arguably Yeats' most famous poem, *Innisfree*.

Richards and *Zen in the Art of Archery*
by Eugen Herrigel.[7] There can be no
substitute for reading and studying both of
these books because understanding the content
is intimately related to the life experiences described
in them. One of the great lessons these books conveyed is that being
able to access one's Center can only be gained through living life *being*
centered. We cannot "go deeper" to get to it; we descend into it
(Center) and then "roots" that sprout from that
"lowered Center" go down into the ground on which we stand to give
it depth. While many artists can acquire some degree of Center, that
Center never gains depth because the final journey of rootedness
into the ground never occurs. A strong connection between
low Center and the earth must not only be perceived, but
also felt. Elaine Brown used words such as "rootedness"
and "deep grounding." If we consider the miracle of a
tree, then we can begin to understand the concept
of "rootedness." In this illustration, it is obvious
that more of the tree is below the ground than
above it! It is that very image which every
artist should conceptualize when musicing,
acting, or dancing.

The most perplexing difficulty with
acquiring and staying in one's Center has to
do with life itself. No matter how well we
learn to physically align and adjust the body

7   In this book, many quotes for the chapters are drawn from another book by Richards, *The Crossing Point*. It
is recommended that readers of this book read the centering book before reading *The Crossing Point*.

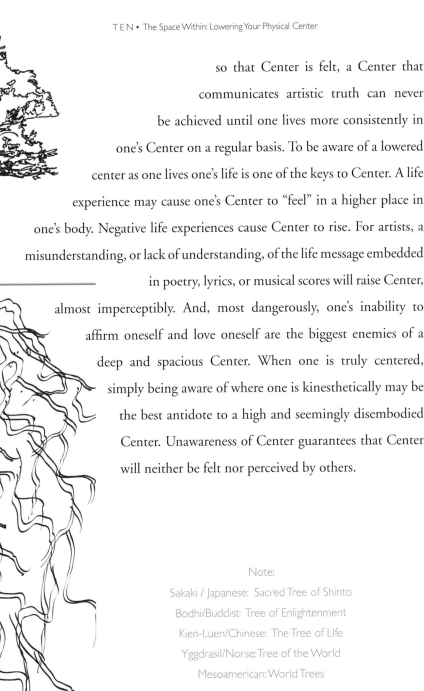

so that Center is felt, a Center that communicates artistic truth can never be achieved until one lives more consistently in one's Center on a regular basis. To be aware of a lowered center as one lives one's life is one of the keys to Center. A life experience may cause one's Center to "feel" in a higher place in one's body. Negative life experiences cause Center to rise. For artists, a misunderstanding, or lack of understanding, of the life message embedded in poetry, lyrics, or musical scores will raise Center, almost imperceptibly. And, most dangerously, one's inability to affirm oneself and love oneself are the biggest enemies of a deep and spacious Center. When one is truly centered, simply being aware of where one is kinesthetically may be the best antidote to a high and seemingly disembodied Center. Unawareness of Center guarantees that Center will neither be felt nor perceived by others.

Note:

Sakaki / Japanese: Sacred Tree of Shinto
Bodhi/Buddist: Tree of Enlightenment
Kien-Luen/Chinese: The Tree of LIfe
Yggdrasil/Norse: Tree of the World
Mesoamerican: World Trees

Center by Association

Some aspects of Center can be acquired through skillful observation and by being in close proximity to centered persons. Spending so much time in the presence of Elaine Brown, both in her choirs and as her assistant in graduate school, was highly influential in my developing awareness of Center. One senses the centeredness of others, and I have found that that centeredness does transfer—as if by "magic." A person who is centered not only affects the person nearest him or her, but is able to transform groups of people by his or her mere ability to "be centered" in the presence of others. It is when one experiences such centeredness that one begins to understand both the power and importance of Center to artistic communication and honest, compelling human expression.

The Paradox of Center

There is another paradox of Center that has been described to me and that I believe to be so. Many years ago when I was lecturing and discussing Center and its importance in one of my conducting classes, a fascinating discussion ensued between a Benedictine monk and two nuns. The monk posed a question to me, which frankly I had difficulty answering. He asked me if my "spiritual" Center, my physical Center, is the same as the place that I pray from? My answer to the question was that they *are* the same. The monk and the two nuns argued that they are *not* the same, and I tend to agree with them. The monk started the discussion by explaining that when one prays, one must move to a "higher" place in one's perceptual system. True prayer, according to that discussion, must move out of Center to what they called "a higher communicative place." Many of us might call that an "out-of-body" place. But one can mesh and connect one's prayerful place and one's Center when performing and teaching. However, to mesh those two states of being requires understanding, awareness, and a deep desire to do so. But they are *two separate realms,* which make us unique as human beings. When those areas are linked through intellect, will, and action, a powerful energy is unleashed. At this point in the text, I propose this idea as an important point for consideration and personal reflection. I will leave it to you, and perhaps others, to add clarity to my premise. But like all theories, it is something that makes sense to me. Consider the following quote from a graduate student paper:

> As you may have discovered from my other paper about philosophies (or will discover if you have not read it), my spirituality plays a large role in my life. Contrary to some thought, I cannot and will not separate my religion from my spirituality no matter how hard I would ever try. My religious beliefs guide me as I travel through this world and they help me become the person I believe I was meant to be.
>
> —from a graduate conducting student essay

This is a troubling statement because it speaks to the complexity of the concept of Center. The inability to separate one's religiosity (as Robert Shaw called it) from one's spirituality, in my opinion, will mute, veil, or muffle one's musical and artistic messages. While the religion that each of us uses (and practices) to make sense out of life, and to provide us with our spirituality (which is essential to the human condition), is important, the spirituality that provides the commonality among all of us as human beings *is* different from our own individual religious beliefs. Yes, Bach's music was deeply influenced by Martin Luther and his beliefs, but as Robert Shaw has so eloquently stated, the Crucifixus of the Mass in B Minor is great not because it is a wonderful depiction of that religious event, but because Bach understood, and wrote into the sound of that work, the enormity of the effect of that event upon all humankind.

Regarding the student quote earlier, bolstered by discussions with religious clerics and theologians, it is not *separation* that we want here, but a coexistence of the two within our artistic selves at different levels. We want the honesty and belief that all religion brings to our human state, but we want our spirituality to live in the same place as our physical Center. To do otherwise would breed intense disconnection not only from self, but from those with whom we are attempting to communicate our artistic/human message. We carry our religious spirituality with us, but we ground ourselves in our human spirituality. This is an important and necessary balance for artists to attain and maintain.

This is a thorny issue to be sure, and my wish is not to offend anyone, but instead ask each person to personally explore this important human dichotomy, even enigma, within him or herself. Some clarity is necessary for our Center to be perceived, as a lack of forethought will cause a blurring of our human message, which will always be manifested by means of a technique that is unique to each of the performing arts.

Recently I asked someone who was associated with a particular orchestra why members of one of the country's finest orchestras intensely disliked their conductor. This maestro had an impressive knowledge of the score and his technique was flawless. However, you could hear in the sound of that orchestra a lack of ensemble and, more importantly, a lack of will. The person with whom I was conversing gave me the most unusual explanation. He said, "The orchestra just doesn't like his mojo!" I laughed, but after some reflection, the issue was actually one of Center. This conductor obviously lacked Center, which disturbed the orchestra in a wordless way. If that conductor had Center, he might have had the "mojo" the orchestra so desperately wanted. Center is a powerful force in musicing. In fact, it has everything to do with the honesty and integrity of both teaching and performing.

Finding, Locating, and Discovering Physical Center

The problem of location described earlier lies not in the fact that we do not have a Center, but that our Center is not "low" enough in our bodies. Center must be a kinesthetic "thing" for us. We must "feel" where it is; it defies description or exact anatomical location.

At the Laban/Bartenieff Institute for Movement Studies in New York, I took a course in the Efforts in Combination: Flow, Weight, Time, and Space. We were lead through a number of exercises in each of those efforts in situations that would allow us to experience, as much as possible, each effort in isolation. The exercise for Weight is still the best way to "re-locate" one's Center— that is, to experience it in its proper "low" position within the body. The exercise on the next page, called the "towel slap," is one of the most important exercises for both discovering Center and for re-locating a Center that is too high.

Towel Slap Exercise

Each student should bring a large, thick towel to class. Students should slap the towel against the floor to obtain the loudest possible sound. As they slap their towels, students should analyze their movement patterns to determine which of the Efforts in Combination produces the loudest towel slap.

The students will find that if they grab the end of the towel and begin the activity with their hands extended backward over the head, bringing the towel directly over the top of the head and following the midline of the body will produce the loudest sound. What the students will experience is a sudden use of weight as the towel is slapped. As the towel slaps to the floor, they should feel the sudden dispersion of weight into the floor.

Important to this exercise are (1) body alignment, (2) beginning and ending locations of the towel, and (3) the focused energy as the towel hits the floor. The diagrams on the pages that follow show the beginning, middle, and final positions of the towel slap.

Figure 10.1. Beginning position for towel slap exercise.

Figure 10.2. Middle position for towel slap exercise.

Figure 10.3. Ending position for towel slap exercise.

The first secret to this exercise is that the student needs to bring the towel through the Center or midline of the body. Then, to make a loud slap with the towel, the body must be in a perfect alignment. The most important part of this exercise is that at the moment the energy is released in the loud slap when the towel meets the floor, the student will feel the "true" location of Center within his or her body. Having experienced the feeling through this exercise, the student can then recall it using "kinesthetic imagination" whenever needed.

Aside from the towel slap exercise above, the following exercises have been equally effective in helping to establish the kinesthetic location of Center.

Tiptoeing Exercise

Tiptoe around the room, making as little sound as possible. What does your body feel like? Where do you feel your Center of levity?

In this tiptoe activity, you most likely feel your Center of levity high in your body. To tiptoe quietly, you actually hold back the displacement of weight as you move, or in other words, you experience lightness, which is a withholding of weight.

This exercise is important because it teaches us what Center is not! When we withhold weight, or avoid sensing weight, our Center rises.

Skipping Exercise

Skipping is one of the most valuable of all movement activities because the entire body is carried by an energy continuum that can only be felt if the body is centered. The constant releasing of energy coupled with a dynamic inertia that centers itself around the core makes this an essential exercise to master.

Perform this activity in an area that allows the use of a large floor space. Begin skipping across the floor. Try to make it across the room with as few skips as possible, skipping as high as possible. As you skip, make certain that the upper body remains free.

What image will help you to skip higher? You will find that the more you can "hold back" your weight at the top or highest point of the skip, the higher you will be able to skip. Where do you feel your Center of levity as you skip?

Tug of War Exercise

Engage in a tug of war with a partner using a long, heavy bath or beach towel. Each participant grasps an end of the towel. Then both count to three and begin the tug. When done correctly, neither partner should win; it should be a standoff. Perform the tug of war again and experiment with the positioning of your body to achieve the lowest possible center of levity (lightness of weight). You will find that a condition of equilibrium occurs when both partners squat in an ape-like position so that their center of levity, or center of weight, drops into the pelvis area. When the condition of equilibrium occurs, where do *you* feel your Center? Do you feel it low in your body? You should "feel" your Center of levity in that "tug-of-war" place when you conduct. If you do, you will find that when you breathe, the air will be able to drop to the same place where you feel your center of levity.

Chakras, Energy Centers, and Center

Center carries a vibrant energy that can be felt and certainly perceived. Aside from locating one's Center, it is important for one to conceptualize that Center is felt within as a source of energy.

The concept of chakra, as understood in Eastern philosophy, does not exist in Western medical science. In Eastern thought, the chakras are thought to be levels of consciousness and energy centers in addition to being states of the soul. "Proving" the existence of chakras is akin to "proving" the existence of a soul, a slightly thorny issue. A mystic deals with these metaphysical concepts on the metaphysical plane, as a model for their individual internal

96

experience, and when they talk about "energy Centers" they are generally referring to subtle, spiritual forces that work on the psyche and spirit, not about physical electrical or magnetic fields.

The primary importance and level of existence of chakras is posited to reside in both the psyche and the spirit, but they are located in different and distinct regions of the body. However, there are those who believe that chakras have a physical manifestation as well. Although there is no evidence that Indian mystics made this association, it is noted by many that there is a marked similarity between positions and roles for chakras, positions and roles of the glands in the endocrine system, and positions of the nerve ganglia (also known as "plexuses") along the spinal column. These correlations open up the possibility that two vastly different systems of conceptualizing the human constitution have been brought to bear in systemizing insights about the same phenomena. Some think chakras are physically manifested in these glands, and they are subjectively manifested in associated psychological and spiritual experiences.

Indeed, the various hormones secreted by these glands do have a dramatic effect on human psychology, and an imbalance of hormones can cause psychological or physiological imbalance in a person. Whether these changes in body state have a bearing on spiritual matters is a subject

Note:

4000-year-old symbol meaning
"Wheel of Life."

Crown Chakra

Third Eye Chakra / Forehead

Throat Chakra

Heart Chakra

Solar Plexus /Navel Chakra

Sacral / Sexual Chakra

Root/Base Chakra

The word Chakra,
means
"wheel," "disc," or "turning"
in Sanskrit.

of dissent even among the Indian theorists, and the different systems of conceptualization, Indian and Western, make only a partial convergence in this case.

The seven main chakras are described as being aligned in an ascending column from the base of the spine to the top of the head. Each chakra is associated with a particular color, multiple specific functions, an aspect of consciousness, a classical element, and other distinguishing characteristics.

The chakras vitalize the physical body and are associated with interactions of both a physical and mental nature. They are considered to be loci of life energy, or prana, which flows through and among the chakras along pathways called *nadis*. This column of chakras begins in the body at Center and moves upward within the core of the body.

Center Resides Deep within the Pelvis

One of the issues with understanding Center is knowing where it "feels" within your body. It is almost impossible to realize Center unless you understand the architecture of the body. You cannot experience Center within the pelvis if you do not have the correct anatomical concept of where the pelvis is! Until the body map is clarified and adjusted with the correct location of the pelvis, chances are very real that your Center will sit "too high" within the body. Following are some imagery exercises to help re-map not only pelvis position, but also Center, which rests in that area.

The Pelvis: The Central Core of the Body

The pelvis has a central role in the postural alignment of conductors, singers, actors, or dancers. The easiest way to learn about the pelvis is to experience it in its correct position. Sit on a hard or firm chair, preferably one with a flat seat. Place your hands with palms upward on the seat and then sit on your hands. Find the two bony protuberances at the bottom of your pelvis and place them directly in your hands. These are known as the *sit bones*. Once you have found the sit bones and have them placed in the palms of your hands, remove your hands and allow those sit bones to directly contact the chair. Allow your feet to rest flat on the floor. Your legs should be relaxed and should be able to swing freely from left to right. The weight of your upper body should rest squarely on those sit bones. Feel the sensation of the pelvis, now in its correct position. Take a deep breath and allow the air to fall low into the pelvis. As an experiment, place your hands under the sit bones again. Tilt the pelvis back slightly. Inhale. Is the depth of the breath as low or free? Probably not! Now roll the pelvis forward. Inhale. Likewise, the breath will not be as low.

Return now to the correct pelvic position. Check that your feet are flat on the floor and that your legs can swing freely from the pelvis. Once the pelvis is aligned by having the sit bones in contact with the chair, stand. As you stand, be certain not to change the relative space between your feet or the position of your pelvis. When this is done correctly, your pelvis will feel wider and open. *Your knees should not be locked, and your body weight should be equally distributed between the balls of your feet and your heels.* This wide and open pelvis is necessary for the good breathing technique that is the most important tool for the performer. Now that you have experienced the correct alignment of the pelvis, it is important that you understand the sensations of incorrect pelvic alignment. Just as you did before, tilt the pelvis slightly forward. What happens? You will find that your knees lock and your weight shifts toward the balls of your feet. You might also feel a forward tipping sensation. Now rotate your pelvis slightly backward. You will notice that your knees again lock, your thighs may become rigid, and your weight shifts to the heels. Now return to your seat. Find your sit bones. Check that your feet are flat on the floor and that your legs swing freely. Stand and once again experience the pelvis in its proper position for breathing, singing, and conducting.

The Interrelationship of the Head and the Spine

Now you have found your appropriate pelvic alignment, but your body alignment is not yet complete. We now need to consider the effect of the head on our alignment. The ability to feel Center is directly related to one's alignment.

Many approaches to the correction of posture do not draw attention to the integral role of the head to our overall body alignment. Consider the following. How much does your head weigh? It might be difficult for you to come up with an accurate answer because of the wonder of our body's architecture. We, as a general rule, do not "feel" the weight of our head because of the engineering of our body. No matter the position of our head, our body compensates for the shifting weight of the head. It is common knowledge that the weight of the head can be from twelve to eighteen pounds. To bring this into focus, the weight of the head is similar to the average weight of a bowling ball. Consider further that weight must balance precariously on the top of the spinal column, which ends in the center of your head between your ears. In Figure 10.4 you can see the fragility (reduced sizing as you ascend toward the head) of the vertebrae as they move into the head.

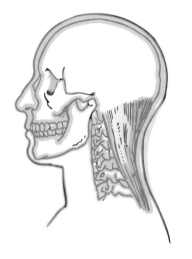

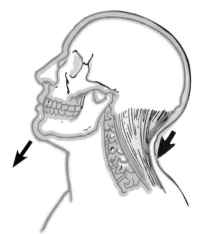

Figure 10.4. Outline of skull and neck vertebrae.

Figure 10.5. Downward pull.

If the head tips slightly (downward pull), then muscles in the back of the neck become tense and short, and attempt to counterbalance the head by taking it backward and downward on the vertebrae. This can be seen in Figure 10.5. This compression of the neck may then result in raised shoulders or the spine curved forward. In turn, this positioning will cause the pelvis to roll forward and the knees to lock. When the body is thus misaligned, breathing becomes increasingly difficult and natural movement response to rhythm, especially in the upper body, is inhibited.

To begin to find your correct alignment, once again find the sit bones. Make the sit bones contact the chair (Figure 10.6). Stand as before. Now think of the sub-occipital muscles at the back of the head as a hand, as shown in Figure 10.7, that gently supports the back of your head off and away from your neck vertebrae.

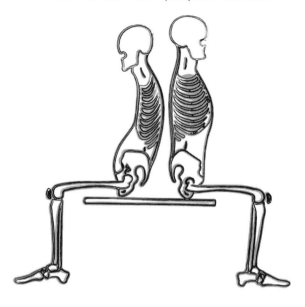

Figure 10.6. Incorrect (left) and correct (right) alignment using sit bones.

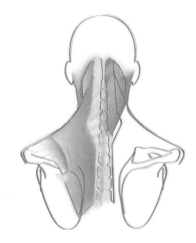

Figure 10.7. Correct body map of head, neck, musculature.

Head misalignment in conductors is most often manifested in the shoulders appearing high and either hunched up towards the ears or pressed forward in an unnatural position. What causes this hunching is the trapezius muscle, which drapes itself downward from the back of the neck, out to the shoulders, and down.

Centering Activities for Musicians, Actors, and Dancers

After becoming sensitive to the Efforts in Combination and to the role of weight in conducting, several Laban exercises can assist you in finding your "gravitational," or energy, Center—that is, your "rootedness" or "grounding." Such a sense of "centeredness" in overall conducting gesture is necessary for evoking a low-seated breath from the choir. Centeredness is a feeling, a state of being. It is directly related to where you feel your weighted Center. The following activities can refamiliarize conductors with their center of levity. The concept of the center of levity is the experience of shifting weight without changing the strength of lightness. Heaviness, in this case, can be thought of as "giving in" to gravity.

Breathing to Center

Eight-Handed Breathing: Understanding Inhalation and Exhalation

The major factor that impedes proper inhalation and exhalation in both conductor and singer is a misconception about how the breath works in an anatomical sense. To remedy this, one very valuable rehearsal technique is to show and explain this breathing process using what is called *Eight-Handed Breathing*.[8]

Central to the understanding of the breathing process is to gain an understanding of what happens anatomically when breath comes into the

---

8   A video version of Eight-Handed Breathing to show to choirs, or for conductor's study and understanding, can be found on the DVD/video: *Body Mapping and Basic Conducting Patterns* by Heather Buchanan and James Jordan (GIA).

body. When breath enters the body, what part of the body moves first, second, third, and fourth? If either the singer or conductor does not understand this process, then unfortunately, neither conductor nor choir will breathe well, and the tone of the choir will be adversely affected.

The Body Mechanics of Breathing

The following are the parts of the body that move in succession when inhalation occurs:

The Inhalation Process

Ribs of the back traverse or travel outward, with each rib traveling at its own rate.

The diaphragm moves from a more-domed to a less-domed position.

The abdominal walls (front and sides) move outward.

The pelvic floor drops slightly.

Note:
Inhalation *always* occurs in the above order with all of the above always participating!

Using the hands as a physical representation of the above, the inhalation sequence would appear as shown in Figure 10.8.

Figure 10.8. Inhalation process.

The Exhalation Process

Ribs of the back traverse or travel inward, with each rib traveling at its own rate.

The diaphragm moves from a less-domed to more-domed position.

The abdominal walls (front and sides) move inward.
The pelvic floor rises slightly.

Note:

It is important to understand that the *order* of movement of the anatomy of the body is the same for exhalation as it is for inhalation. Many conductors and singers believe that, anatomically, the exhalation process is the reverse of the inhalation process. This is a perceptual fantasy. Correction of this misconception will dramatically improve the tone and expressivity of any ensemble.

Using the hands as a physical representation of the above, the exhalationsequence would appear as shown in Figure 10.9.

Figure 10.9. Exhalation process.

Eleven
Your Architectural Center:
The Importance of the Dimensional Cross of Axis

James Jordan

Understanding the Architecture of the Body
to Accurately Locate and Perceive Your Core

One of the challenges for anyone studying music, dance, or theater is to not only gain an awareness of the body but to also acquire a geometric perception, if you will, of the space that the body occupies and how the body moves within that space. Geometric perception of how one's body is organized around its core or center is pivotal to gaining an understanding of Center. Leonardo da Vinci was fascinated by the symmetries that occupy the body in his rendering of the Vitruvian Man standing in both a square and a circle (see Figure 11.1). He was preoccupied with Plato's idea that in three-dimensional space there are only five regular and perfect solids or crystalline figures in all of nature. Using the ideas of both Plato and da Vinci, Rudolf von Laban made a profound mark on dance education and the world of dance through his system of dance notation and the vocabulary he developed to accurately describe the complex world of movement. Like da Vinci, Laban envisioned the geometric space surrounding our bodies. He named that geometric shape (as represented by the icosahedron) the *kinesphere*. The icosahedron is, in effect, a cognitive map of the parameters of our movement, a representation of all of our personal space. Without that map firmly in his or her perception, an expressive artist can never achieve a full range of movement based upon body use. The perception of the space that one occupies in all its dimensions empowers and expands the possibilities of human expression.

Figure 11.1. Leonardo da Vinci, The Vitruvian Man.

The Sound Membrane or Door Plane

Laban, when discussing the geometric delineations of the space in which we move, defined one of the planes as a door plane. Imagine a vertical surface in front of you that is similar to the height and width of a door and at a comfortable welcoming distance from your body; Laban called that imaginary vertical surface a *door plane*. The artist, however, must not envision that door plane as a solid mass but rather as a flexible large membrane that represents the sound itself.

It is important to conceptualize the vertical plane, or what I call the "membrane plane," directly in front of you. In Figure 11.2, the line on the illustration represents a wall that can be likened to a flexible membrane representing sound. By visualizing such a vertical plane, you can begin to establish a direct connection with the sound or spoken word and an intimate connection with audiences or ensembles.

Figure 11.2. Side view of embrace
with the sound membrane or door plane.

Simultaneous Planes: The Three Dimensional Planes

The person who has learnt to relate himself to Space, and has physical mastery of this, has Attention. The person who has mastery of his relation to the Weight factor of effort has Intention and he has Decision when he is adjusted to Time. Attention, intention and decision are the stages of inner preparation of an outer bodily action. This comes about when through the Flow of movement, effort finds concrete expression in the body. (p. 251)

–Rudolf von Laban
Laban for All by Jean Newlove and John Dalby

Perception, or rather a constant and intimate awareness of personal space, must be everything to a performing artist. Awareness of body, awareness of the space in which you move, and awareness of sound all must function simultaneously. To acquire this comprehensive awareness, you must *want* to acquire it. Awareness is truly a state that must be desired to be acquired. Of all the awarenesses that can be problematic for performing artists, *space* poses the most serious perceptual problems. However, once understood, performances can achieve fluidity, breadth, and expansiveness.

The illustration in Figure 11.3 depicts in three dimensions the three planes—as conceptualized by Laban and generalized by this author—that must be part of a performer's geometric perceptual apparatus at all times. One of Laban's unique gifts was to be able to summarize all movement possibilities into what he called a "dimensional cross" (shown below). The vertical plane should be perceived as the points of balance that are organized from head to toe in the internal Center of the body—like a vertical rod at the body's exact geographic center. The horizontal, or table plane, is the line of ictus.

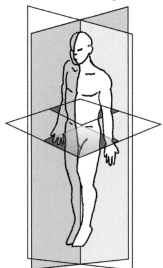

Figure 11.3. The three-dimensional planes.

Once self-perception of these three planes is completed, it is important for artists to not only perceive those planes in front of them, but to also understand that the planes cut through them to behind them. When this is in place, the body's farthest points of exterior boundaries form a twenty-faced geometric figure called the *icosahedron* (see Figure 11.4). It is important for performers to perceive the space in front of them as well as all of the space around them that forms the area for movement. The icosahedron represents all space possible for movement. An active awareness of the icosahedron around one establishes within oneself and with one's audience the strong and alive perception of one's geometric center. Without the establishment in one's self-perception of this organizational geometry, one's spiritual center will never have a home that can be read by an audience or other artists.

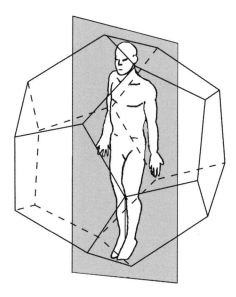

Figure. 11.4. Icosahedron with door plane highlighted.

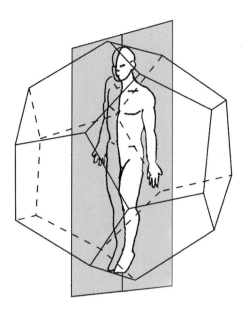

Figure. 11.5. Icosahedron with wheel plane highlighted.

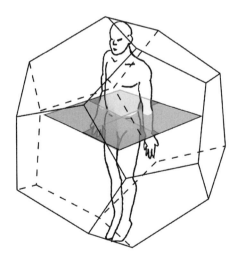

Figure. 11.6. Icosahedron with table plane highlighted.

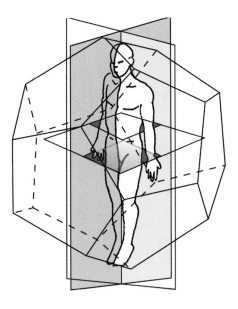

Figure. 11.7. Icosahedron showing all three planes.

Twelve

Another Paradigm for Physical Center: Core-Distal Connectivity

James Jordan

Total Body Connectivity: The whole body is connected, and all parts are in relationship. Change in one part changes the whole. Acknowledging relationship between parts of the body brings the possibility for both differentiation of the parts and integration of the whole. (p. 39)

Frequently, as movement becomes more complex, movers "forget" that their whole body is connected and begin trying to "stick their limbs into the right places" to fulfill tasks in a sort of helter-skelter way, without any organizing framework. Connective pathways seem broken. Limbs seem to fly away or get left behind, no longer connected to the alive action. When this happens, it is important to return again to simple movement and spend time rediscovering that the whole body can be organized by a pattern of connectivity that begins in the center of the core of the body and radiates out through the torso to the proximal joints, the mid-limbs and all the way to the distal ends of the extremities. (pp. 67–68)

Because the navel center is where the "guts" are located, a person might use the phrase, "I know it in my guts," "It goes to the gut," or "In my gut I love, hate, accept, reject, etc." That aspect of what is "Gut Truth" for the person is usually expressed with a movement that comes into or goes away from the body's core. (p. 82)

It is also the heart of the fight-or-flight response—the body's ability to organize all limbs at once, in relation to center, and act instantaneously. In truth, this pattern of movement we have explored…sets up a basic pattern of "Twoness" (as opposed to "oneness" in the Breath Pattern). Here are a few of the polarities that could be explored:

Me–Not Me	Acceptance–Rejection
In–Out	Gather–Scatter
Towards–Away	Inside–Outside
Take In–Give Out	Receptive–Expressive (p. 82)

—Peggy Hackney
Making Connections

Body connectivity is one of the most important concepts for a conductor to understand and master. This connectivity provides artists with another perceptual tool for visualization of one's Center. Additionally, I have found that the concept of core-distal connectivity is central to establishing meaningful expressive movement.[9]

So many times, I have observed performing artists who had great conducting facility, and in fact good coordinative skills, but there was something missing. Generally, when this lack of cohesion in the movement was detected, I would always advise becoming more "grounded," more "connected to the

---

[9] The work of Peggy Hackney in the book *Making Connections: Total Body Integration through Bartenieff Fundamentals* was a pivotal resource for this material. The reader is encouraged to read and study this comprehensive text.

earth," or more "centered." While all those concepts improved the gesture, or movement, there was always something eluding the pedagogy. There was an important connection that the artist needed to establish between Center and his or her groundedness. Center establishes a certain rootedness that gives some integrity to the artistic movement. When one's perception is clarified, Center and groundedness become a given rather than an exception in this pedagogical approach. But the truth of any conducting gesture ultimately lies in its spiritual core and the connectedness to that "inside" and "physical" center to the hands through the arms via one's body. The concept that clearly connects and relates all movement into a functioning whole is the powerful concept of *distal connection.*

Connecting Core to the Distal Relationships of the Body

Performing artists function in the world of distal connections. If their movement is to have any meaning to the ensemble, they must somehow connect their "extremities" (i.e., hands via the arms) to their core. Alexander Technique has taught us imagery that allows for a more direct connection of the arms to the core of the body.[10] For example, Alexander Technique has taught us to perceive that our arms have no joints and they connect to our bodies in the small of the back. While this image is extremely valuable in connecting our arms to our bodies, it generally is unable to ultimately connect our arms to the *core* of our bodies. Until that connection to core is made, gesture cannot be empowered to communicate directly to any ensemble, other artists, or an audience.

---

10   This is assuming the artist has correctly mapped him or herself using the principles of Body Mapping. Fundamental to all expressive gesture is an intimate understanding of one's body map as presented in the *Evoking Sound* DVD (Buchanan/Jordan) and the principles set forward in *The Anatomy of Conducting* DVD (GIA). These principles about how the body is organized can be generalized to the movement needs of the performing artist.

The Starfish Connection

To understand this principle, envision the structure of your expressive body as a starfish. Orient the starfish in your mind with one point at the top and the other points being both arms and legs. Starfish move distally; that is, all of their locomotion grows *out of* their center, or rather *through* their center.[11] And the starfish moves through what Laban calls a *dimension cross of axis.* That is, the upper right hand should always be perceived

Note:

Elder Futhark runic alphabet: meaning "gift," sacrifice, generosity, and balance.

as being connected with the lower left foot passing through the core of the body. The upper left hand should always be perceived as being connected to the lower right foot, establishing a connection to the core of the body by passing through it. Many performers perceive their own movement as each arm connected to the trunk of their body. Their legs are attached in similar fashion to the trunk of the body. Because of this misconception, the limbs, especially the arms, appear to the choir as moving appendages. Visually, this concept of the "X" distal connection of opposite limbs can be depicted as shown in Figure 12.1.

---

11   I wish to thank Lisa Billingham of James Madison University for introducing me to this concept.

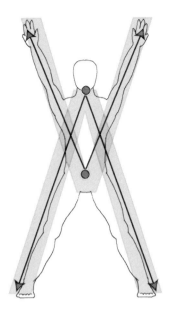

Figure 12.1.
X distal connection of opposite limbs.

The Second Dimension of Connectivity

Another valuable image concerns not the physical connections of the body, but the energy flow through the body outward to the ensemble. Barbara Conable, in her Body Mapping classes, frequently quotes the somatic principle: "The choir will perceive only what you perceive." Broadened a bit, the statement could also be interpreted as "the audience will perceive only what you perceive." Conable always stated this principle when referring to the idea that if you are aware of your body and how it is constructed, then the choir will instantaneously perceive knowledge.

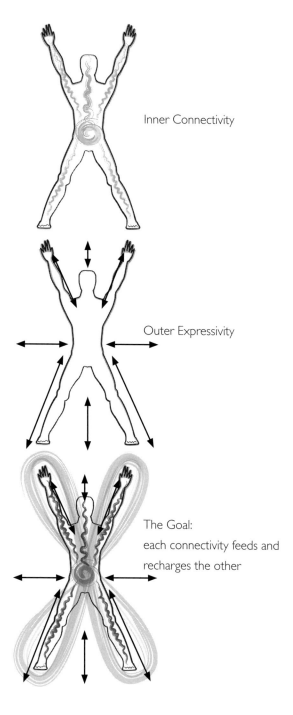

Inner Connectivity

Outer Expressivity

The Goal:
each connectivity feeds and
recharges the other

Figure 12.2. Energy flow

The same principle applies to energy flow. Peggy Hackney in her book *Making Connections,* uses the imagery in Figure 12.2 to discuss what she terms a "dynamic sense of alignment" (p. 101). However, the same image can be effectively used for artists in a discussion of how energy flows through the core of the body. This energy flow creates a dynamic energy pathway through the body that will be perceived by the audience and other artists if the performer perceives his or her energy pathways in this way. One need only be vulnerable and open for that energy to be transmitted in a direct, one-to-one fashion to each member of the ensemble or audience. That "energy flow" can be further generalized to one's grounding to the earth and connection of one's core to the ground.

Thirteen

Center as the Focus of Connection Between Artist and Ensemble or Artist and Audience

James Jordan

The center that I cannot find is known to my unconscious mind.
(p. 85)

—W. H. Auden
The Artist's Way by Julia Cameron

The relationships between performers and their instruments and performers and their audiences can create a dilemma. This aspect of a performer's presence in front of their audience is often neglected in lessons due to emphasis on what is perceived to be basic technique. What I have found is that unless the lesson includes work on presence, as much as 40 percent of tone quality can be missing. (p. 848)

The first prerequisite for presence in performance is focusing on the musical message rather than yourself. Often I have to remind students that the message is far more important than the performer. The passion and enthusiasm of the music must be fueled by a genuine desire of the performer to be there. (p. 851)

—Meribeth Bunch
"Are you all there?"
The Strad, August 2002

The condition of being human can obviously be as large or as small as the human being chooses it to be… (p. 11)

—Daniel Barenboim

Music Quickens Time

Well, and what is freedom? First of all, freedom seems to mean the absence of external restraint, the freedom to play. When we are free from external tyrannies, we seek freedom from our inner limitations. We find that in order to play we must be nimble and flexible and imaginative, we must be able to have fun, we must *feel* enjoyment, and sometimes long imprisonment has made us numb and sluggish. And then we find out that there are, paradoxically, disciplines which create in us capacities which allow us to seek our freedom. We learn how to rid ourselves of boredom, of stiffness, our repressed anger, our anxiety. We become brighter, more energy flows through us, our limbs rise, our spirit comes alive in our tissues. (p. 22)

—Mary Caroline Richards

Centering

There is a vitality, a life force, an energy, a quickening, that is translated through you into action, and because there is only one of you in all time, this expression is unique. And if you block it, it will never exist through any other medium and will be lost. (p. 75)

—Martha Graham

The Artist's Way by Julia Cameron

An act of the self, that's what one must make. An act of the self, from me to you. From center to center. We must mean what we say, from our innermost heart to the outermost galaxy. Otherwise we are lost and dizzy in a maze of reflections. We carry light within us. There is no need merely to reflect. Others carry light within them. These lights must wake each other. My face is real. Yours is. Let us find our way to our initiative. (p. 18)

—Mary Caroline Richards

Centering

He [Edward Said] also knew how to distinguish clearly between power and force, which constituted one of the main ideas of his struggle. He knew quite well that, in music, force is not power, something which many of the world's political leaders do not perceive. The difference between power and force is equivalent to the difference between volume and intensity in music. When one speaks with a musician and says to him, "You are not playing intensely enough," his first reaction is to play louder. And it is exactly the opposite: the lower the volume, the greater need for intensity, and the greater the volume, the greater the need for a calm force in the sound. (pp. 127–128)

—Daniel Barenboim

Music Quickens Time

Images and fantasy are important parts of any performing artist's life. In fact, those fantasies and images are central to the creative process. Fantasies about the color of sounds, the emphasis and inherent color of a stressed word, whether spoken or sung, all enter into one's world of fantasy that is central to the creative process. But equally important to the creative process is how one believes, or rather perceives, how one's energy is transferred to an ensemble or audience. The clarity of one's "fantasy" about this has everything to do with both the effectiveness and impact upon musicing, acting, performing, or moving.

One of the most important images I acquired from Elaine Brown is the importance of visualizing Center after having done the hard work of locating it through many different awarenesses. Center is clarified through both spiritual channels and physical location or, in some cases, relocation lower in the body.

It is necessary to envision Center as a vital energy source that can emit energy outward towards others. Moreover, that energy needs to be released in a focused form. If you imagine that the energy from Center moves from your body in the shape of a cone, then your energy has a focal point immediately in front of the ensemble. Similarly, if you perceive that the energy of an ensemble (or audience) can likewise be focused, the convergence of both of these very powerful forces converges at a point between the two. It is in that incredible intersection where both communication and, most importantly, connection happen. To use the words of Martin Buber, that point is the point at which "I and Thou" become the same. In this paradigm, musical and artistic communication then becomes a direct 1:1 process between the performing artist and a group of "receivers" in the artistic creativity process.

To become aware of Center, and to *stay* aware of it, is one of the great gifts for any performer. A very real sense of Center provides an unmistakable energy for all things creative. Center becomes a volatile, incendiary device that can ignite the forward motion of a musical phrase or color the most complex harmonic structure.

The visualization of this principle is stupendously simple. Staying aware of Center is an ongoing challenge. But as the saying goes, "It is all about the visualization." In a sense, this example is a way of clearly mapping the energy center or energy core in your own body, and further mapping how that energy exits your body and connects with others. (Figure 13.1 illustrates this concept.) The most important point in the illustration is the dot that shows the intersection of the two energy centers. It is important to perceive and believe that those energies truly do have a focal point where those energies meet in a vibrant place in front of us. That point then becomes the point where communication and connection both exist and live in a vibrant and exciting way.

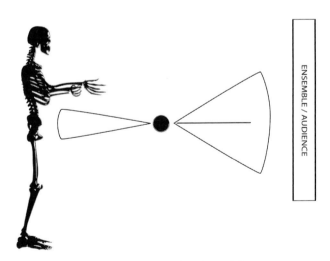

Figure 13.1. Paradigm for location of Center
and role in the creative process.

Fourteen

The Willful Artist:
Moving Through Your Center and Outward

James Jordan

What is important is not to define, but to act. One must try to do one's work with enough love and enough care to make it represent one's very best. The whole joy of being a human being is to realize the difficulty in reaching one's aim. The higher the aim, the higher the difficulty, and the greater our humility and joy. As for beauty—is it not mainly through beauty for service, of which there is no material reward or punishment, that we reach the spiritual art of our life which is the whole purpose of existence and its only goal? (p. 67)

We are often mistaken about art. Art is not emotion. Art is the medium in which emotion is expressed. (p. 77)

You must remember what St. Thomas Aquinas said to play this work.

To be aware of what is going on, one must feel the presence of the past, the presence of the presence, and the presence of the future.

To be this work, you must be its beginning, center and end all at once. Pay attention to all of it. (p. 79)

—Nadia Boulanger

Master Teacher: Nadia Boulanger by Don G. Campbell

Music is what wakes within you when
You are reminded by the instruments.
It is not the violins and the horns, not
The oboe nor the pounding drums.
Nor the melody of the baritone who sings his sweet song.
Nor that of the men's chorus nor that of
The women's chorus.
Music is nearer and farther than these.

—Walt Whitman

Leaves of Grass

Only connect! That was the whole of her sermon. Only connect the prose and the passion, and both will be exalted, and human love will be seen at its height. Live in fragments no longer. Only connect, and the beast and the monk, robbed of the isolation that is life to either, will die. (p. 168)

…railway termini. They are our gates to the glorious and the unknown. Through them we pass out into adventure and sunshine, to them, alas! we return. (p. 28)

—E. M. Forster

Howards End, edited by Alistair M. Duckworth

"Life" wrote a friend of mine, "is a public performance on the violin, in which you must learn the instrument as you go along." (p. 155)

—E. M. Forster

A Room with a View

Hell is a place where nothing connects with nothing. (p. 45)

—Vartan Gregorian citing Dante

Five Minds for the Future by Howard Gardner

I believe, then, that spirit in music is not the wholesale emotional orgasm that weeps appropriately in public, but rather the marshalling of one's keenest, most critical intellectual and moral forces to the point of complete consciousness—'til one hears in terms of values and the movements of the values, until the most pedestrian minutiae of pitch and rhythm are heard inwardly in relation to adjacent minutiae; and finally to the relation to the wholes of form, tonality and intent. (p. 6)

—Robert Shaw

The Robert Shaw Reader

This text has been about preparing for an event for which, in reality, there is no way to prepare. One can merely make ready for this encounter with human spirits in an artistic collaboration where each of those spirits has a deep desire not only to be listened to and heard, but in some small way to connect with each other, and perhaps to a larger world. It is not foolishness to consider the rehearsal and all its preparations as a grand journey each day— that journey being the corporate entity we call a choir, laden with life and with its own desire to speak and be heard.

Creativity Misunderstood: Individual versus Group

For performing artists to delve deeper into the rehearsal process and rehearsal psyche, an essential paradigm shift is necessary, especially if we are to make any progress with understanding our personal rehearsal and preparation techniques and the psychologies employed in the deployment of that technique to an ensemble. Much of the focus within music education and training of musicians has been on defining and understanding the creative process in individuals. We have studied how individuals learn, and we have developed progressive methods which, in reality, deal with teaching individuals disguised as a group. Group musicianship and group creativity are assumed to be the natural outgrowths of individual musicians herded together in an ensemble. Not true. Recent educational excitement around critical pedagogy has taken our eye off the ball. While we need to consider individuals and the experiences they bring to musicing, are not those individual "characteristics" transformed and even mutated when they are in a group setting? How do an individual's experiences translate when they become part of a larger corporate experience? Is the power of the group more powerful than the individuals within it? Moreover, how does all this impact the individual psyche of any performing artist?

Rethinking Personal Rehearsal Preparation: From Personal Practice to Group

For better or worse, rehearsals with other performing artists are group sport. Truman Capote once remarked that he preferred writing novels to plays because he didn't enjoy group sports. The problem with anyone's rehearsal technique is that we have not examined how individual creativity and music learning changes when it is in an ensemble. We all know that it does. But it is for that precise reason that, at times, the right rehearsal technique, or ways to rehearse and prepare for rehearsals, eludes us. It eludes us because we craft our rehearsals thinking about how to teach individuals rather than groups. Or worse yet, we craft rehearsals as if we were

t e a c h i n g

ourselves, rather than our students. In case you haven't noticed, groups are more difficult! Working with other performing artists in a haphazard way can pull us out of the Center we have worked so hard to understand and establish within both our minds and bodies.

West African (Cloth)
BOA ME NA ME
MMOA WO
"Help me and
let me help you."

133

Howard Gardner, in his book, *Five Minds for the Future* (2006) makes this observation. Despite the fact that we have sliced and diced the studies of how individuals learn, we have come to very little understanding of how creativity is transformed in the group setting. Our problems in rehearsals become obstacles because not only are we under-prepared in our basic score-learning processes, but we create problems in our rehearsals because we fail to understand how groups of persons (ensembles) create and *learn* together. Rehearsal technique, to paraphrase Capote, *is* group sport. To not consider the power of creative beings gathered into one place for a common cause may be a bit foolhardy. But to not shape all our pedagogy around the psychology of group creativity has been a terrible misstep. We may have subliminally considered this, but the psychology of the creative process of the group has not informed and directed our pedagogical focus. For anyone interested in rehearsing well, constant re-examination of this powerful community of creative beings must be considered and deeply studied. Martin Buber understood the human potential that was unlocked when persons are in community.

Group creative powers never stagnate unless allowed to through poor rehearsal technique and inadequate score study. Hence, group rehearsal technique or ensemble rehearsal technique, while made up of the same basic building blocks and method, must constantly change because the ensemble is constantly changing…almost from rehearsal to rehearsal! To further compound the issue, how do we as conductors and performing artists in other settings for dance or the theater transform individual listening skills into listening skills that happen within a group through our rehearsal technique?

We all know that ensembles and groups of performing artists need to be taught well, and we all must bury ourselves in the myriad of preparations that will help us find the keys that will open any one of a number of magical musical doors that present themselves at each rehearsal. Aside from learning "the music," we must be able to allow rehearsals to transform into life-nourishing and life-giving experiences. No matter what the choir is—church choir, college choir, middle school choir—if done well, we should all leave the rehearsal better people than when we walked in the door.

Great music can be viewed as an "excuse" for this deep exploration without any further justification. Music provides us with the vehicle to explore all facets of life and can, if taught well, bring us to understandings through sound that words alone simply cannot accomplish. The fact is, while preparation and score study readies one to enter a rehearsal room, no book can ever prepare one for the spontaneity and sparks of the rehearsal room. It seems that in the best of rehearsals, the unexpected appears, and it is only because of preparation and experience that an answer to the musical issue at hand also miraculously appears.

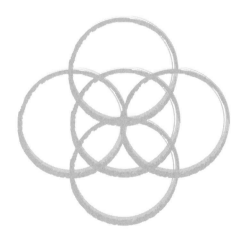

Note:
Celtic Wheel of Being.
The Four Elements are united by Balance, the Fifth Element.

Fifteen

The Dualities of Center

James Jordan

Is this knotted fist of a voice a clue to next year? In the midst of uncertainty in your business life, your love life, your *life* life, your love life, why is Sinatra's voice such a foghorn—such confidence in nervous times allowing you romance but knocking your rose-tinted glasses off your nose, if you get too carried away.

A call to believability.

A voice that says, "Don't lie to me now."…

Fabulous, not fabulist. Honesty to hang your hat on….

Singers, more than other musicians, depend on what they know—as opposed to what they don't want to know about the world. While there is a danger in this—the loss of naïveté, for instance, which holds certain power—interpretative skills generally gain in the course of a life well abused….

To what end? Duality, complexity. I was lucky to duet with a man who understood duality, who had the talent to hear two opposing ideas in a single song, and the wisdom to know which side to reveal at the moment.

This is our moment. What do we hear?

—Bono

"Notes from the Chairman," The New York Times
January 11, 2009

It might be surprising to find this chapter beginning with a quote from the popular artist Bono talking about Frank Sinatra. But I have found that great artists understand one of the characteristics of Center that can at times be elusive.

While many of us would agree that it is important for the art we make to reflect, and perhaps even embody, life experience, there is also the side of musicing that demands a more simple and direct voice. When do we insert our own lives into the composer's or author's voice? Are there times when it is best to just allow simplicity and directness to speak? By being aware of these two extremes, we can know yet another aspect of Center. This aspect of Center, in many ways, is an awareness that by knowing both extremes we can, as artists, select what the musical or artistic statement demands.

Many of us have been taught that by bringing life experience to our music, in so doing we deepen the interpretation. Bringing life experiences to our art causes us to connect with the composer or author in a very real way. But we also need to be aware of when the composer or author voice demands a more simple, direct voice (that the author's voice is strong enough). The dilemma for the artist is how to move between these extremes. To do so is to be aware of both extremes at a place that also lives in our Center. Leonard Bernstein used to speak of "becoming Mahler" when he conducted Mahler, and Igor Stravinsky, the neo-classicist, talked of expressivity as being, at times, not expressive. So where is the balance? It is this strange duality, and the awareness of it, that defines this peculiar aspect of Center.

The artist must be able to allow the composer's voice to be heard and decide which vehicles will speak most directly to the audience. Such is the stuff of interpretation. As Bono says (above), the sound should be a call to believability. This believability is born out of an awareness of Center that is counterbalanced by these dualities.

Mood versus Emotion

If one believes in an honest message as a performer, then one should also be concerned with things that may interfere with that message.

> I believe that moods are what Stephen Jay Gould called a "spandrel," something that is not itself adaptive or useful to our species, but that arises as a by-product of something else that is. My claim is that moods are not useful to us; they filter what we see in the world, and they make us respond on the basis of a narrow if not distorted view of reality. Although I do not think we could live without emotions, I suggest we would lead better lives if we had no moods at all, and were therefore more responsive to what is actually happening in the world rather than what we can see through the narrow filter of one or another mood. (p. 13)

> In terms of this distinction between emotions and moods, to me what is fundamental about a mood is that it lasts a long time—though usually not for weeks, just for hours—and we do not see the world the way we would if we were not in that mood. It distorts and narrows our responses. Therefore it is not good for us. (p. 14)

—The Dalai Lama and Paul Ekman

Emotional Awareness

Whether we perform from either side of this duality of life versus simplicity, our mood can cloud and make extremely murky the voice of what we are performing. While human emotions do play into what we do as artists, we must be aware that our *moods* have great power to deny us not only of being honest messengers of the messages we carry, but also keep us from the stability of Center. To be aware of one's mood is one of the most important awarenesses that one can develop. Mood can move a person out of Center into a place where musical perspective can be veiled or muted. Mood can also gain us access to our own emotional and life experience resources to bring to musicing.

Note:
Another symbol of duality:
Mayan Hunab Ku
Symbol-One
Giver of Movement
and Measure.
Also known as the "Galactic
Butterfly" representing
Universal Consciousness.

An Increased Importance of Awareness

The perspective that an artist can use in performance—that is, the believability factor—is often the result of personal awarenesses in the moment. One example has always reminded me of an artist who understood this balance of duality: Robert Shaw. I observed Mr. Shaw rehearsing the Westminster Symphonic Choir on the Samuel Barber *Prayers of Kierkegaard*. The opening of the work has an extended chant for the lower voices of the choir. After hearing it for the first time, he asked the choir to sing it more simply. After the second try, he asked the choir to sing it "anonymously." The change in the sound was simply amazing. Mr. Shaw changed the human balance within choral sound from overt expression to another aesthetic on the other side of our artistic "duality" towards a more simple, direct, and honest expression of the score. That was a change he decided was necessary for the composer's voice to be heard. His decision represents the decision that all artists must make: the decision of perspective.

Toward Decisions on Artistic Perspective

Center is where true artistic perspective lives. It is clear that we must be aware of both ends of the decision-making process to live in the center of both. If we decide not to be "expressive," then we make that decision in full awareness of the experiences that could be brought to bear on that artistic moment or situation. Sometimes, especially in musicing, it is necessary to allow the voice of author or composer to speak in his or her own voice without clouding the message with personal viewpoint. Other times, actually many times, we make the decision to shuttle between the two, as the expressive element requires. Do we tell the story, or do we allow the story to tell itself? Are we ourselves the story being told, are we observers of the story from a distance, or are we simple "reporters" or "tellers" of the story? Being aware of all of these roles allows us to anchor our Center in real life and allows us the artistic flexibility to move expressively between the three. Eugene Corporon often says, with reference to conductors, that it is our ability to move "expressively between the symbols" that not only gives us our authentic musical voice, but actually clearly defines our expressive center. We must move without resistance between symbol and sound so that an honest voice, a voice that lives within our true Center, is radiantly apparent to others.

The art of non-resistance. One gives up the persona, as Yeats would say, and takes up the mask. That is to say, one becomes that which one is not. Free where one is bound. The physics is clear. The way to center is by abandonment. (p. 141)

—Mary Caroline Richards

Centering

Sixteen

Stabilizing Center:
Humility and Acquiring a Sense of Inner Sacredness

James Jordan

When imagination is allowed to move to deep places, the sacred is revealed. The more different kinds of thoughts we experience around a thing and the deeper our reflections go as we are arrested by its artfulness, the more fully its sacredness can emerge. (p. 289)

As poets and painters of centuries have tried to tell us, art is not about the expression of talent or the making of pretty things. It is about the preservation and containment of soul. It is about arresting life and making it available for contemplation. (p. 303)

"Soul" is not a thing, but a quality or a dimension of experiencing life and ourselves. It has to do with depth, value, relatedness, heart and personal substance. (p. 5)

Observance of the soul can be deceptively simple. You take back what has been disowned. You work with what is, rather than with what you wish were there. (p. 9)

—Thomas Moore

Care of the Soul

After a long life in stillness, you find a joy which is without cause. (p. 34)

If before you have entered into the city of humility, you observe in yourself that you have found rest from the importunity of the passions, do not believe it… You will not find rest from your toil, nor will you have relief from the enemy's treacherous designs, until you reach the abode of holy humility. (p. 41)

—Isaac the Syrian

Isaac the Syrian: An Approach to His World
by Archimandrite Vasileios

This is why, in an act of imitation, every afternoon that I am at home finds me in my backyard for fifteen minutes tending to what has become the fourth component of my daily spiritual practice. For as long as I can remember that practice begins, on arising, with hatha yoga for the body, a reading from a religious classic for my mind, and a blend of prayer and meditation for my spirit. Those three practices remain in place, but it helps to have them grounded, and that is what the addition of composting accomplishes. Being physically anchored to the earth helps us to keep my ego from bobbing along mindlessly on the sea of life. (p. 210)

—Huston Smith

The Way Things Are

It came to me that the soul is like a castle made exclusively of diamond or some other very clear crystal. In this castle are a multitude of dwellings, just as in heavens there are many mansions. (p. 35)

—Saint Teresa of Avila

The Interior Castle

Always the wish that you may find patience enough in yourself
to endure, and simplicity enough to believe; that you may acquire
more and more confidence in that which is difficult, and in your
solitude among others. (p. 120)

—Rainer Maria Rilke

Walking in This World by Julia Cameron

Note:

DWENNIMMEN "Rams Horns"
West African Andinkra Symbol for Humility and Strength. A ram fights his foes,
yet he submits to slaughter (implying that strength also needs humility).

Perhaps the most difficult challenge for anyone in the arts is both acquiring and living within humility. Yet without humility living in a quiet place within us, our art can find no real and true voice. The difficulty with humility is that it becomes so entwined with the negative aspects of one's ego.

Artists who occupy the role of chief "evoker" in a musical situation must work to *not* bring ego into the room. Yet some musicians do so daily. They talk about connecting with their ensembles and audiences and, even through the sheer force of their personalities, literally "will" the music to life. Such music making typically contains the hallmarks of being exciting and rhythmic, but a look beneath the surface reveals an atmosphere that is restrictive and controlled for the art. Connections to the ensemble are thrust upon the ensemble through force of ego. I have seen and heard performances where the music seemed forced upon us through a tour-de-force of ego.

What is ultimately desirable is an artist who understands that by making him or herself less, the music becomes more—more musically and more spiritually. Making yourself (or perhaps more accurately stated, making your ego) less is a challenging if not difficult process. Will and ego, over time, are ultimately dehumanizing to persons housing it and to those who are forced to experience it. Moreover, psychological oppression that is thrust upon those who experience the art of others will never allow for the birth of a compassionate atmosphere in the classroom or the rehearsal room. Ego, or the constant presence of "I," will inhibit compassion, a necessary energy for musicing.

When one has "located" a physical sense of Center, that Center can only be illuminated and transferred to others from a state of silence and calm. The ability to achieve silence within is, perhaps, the secret weapon of a great artist. When right, one's interior is devoid of anything but spaciousness that is occupied in a very real way by love and care. A former student, who is enjoying a great career as a tenor, wrote an account of his move to Maine in order to center himself. He told of taking up jewelry as a craft and related how creating jewelry seemed to center him, calm him, and give him a better place from which to sing.

In a sense, humility within Centeredness can be labeled as a type of "emptiness"; that is, being centered is the lack of other stuff being present within to move one off Center. The quote on the next page defines dramatically what Center should be. Assuming that one is physically centered, the anchoring spirituality that accompanies it, indeed, is the absence of things that make Center murky. Center is a place of vibrant clarity, and that clarity can only be achieved by making other qualities decidedly absent from Center.

Spiritual emptiness is not only an open mind but also an open self. We have to get ourselves out of the way—our explanations, our goals, our habits, and our anxieties. We often try to avoid disaster and fill life with order and meaning, but just as often life unravels all of our careful preparations. (p. 10)

—Thomas Moore

The Soul's Religion

…Psychologically, emptiness is the absence of neurosis, which is essentially an interfering with the unfolding of life and the desires of the deep soul. Various neuroses, such as jealously, inferiority, and narcissism, are nothing more than anxious attempts to prevent life from happening, and when emptied, they transform into their opposites: Jealousy empty of ego is passion. Inferiority empty of ego is humility. Narcissism empty of ego is love of one's soul. We could understand our struggles with these emotions as an invitation to emptiness. The point is not to get rid of them but to let them get rid of us. (pp. 13–14)

—Thomas Moore
The Soul's Religion

Inner Sacredness

Center, which is imbued with the qualities previously described, becomes not only a calm core within Center, but a place where we can feel a calm within that is unmistakable; and out of that place our real voice emerges. That voice emerges with clarity and spontaneity, honesty and deeply human communication. Once acquired, this place must be protected from invasions by the harshness of the world in which we live. The warmth that is generated within us by these qualities has everything to do with our artistic message and the intensity of our ability to connect with others. Center becomes not only a *place* within us, but also a real *feeling* within us. Center, then, by definition, is a place where our physical selves and spiritual presences cohabitate, and it is a place that our body knows and our spirit needs. Center is the baseline out of which all musicing happens. More importantly, once acquired, this inwardly sacred place is a "thing" we must acquire and enter into daily. Once established as the "home base" of all our artistic thoughts and actions, our communication and ability to connect increases tenfold and gives each of us an unmistakable and powerful voice.

The purpose of art is not the release of a momentary ejection of adrenalin, but is, rather, the gradual, lifelong construction of a state of wonder and serenity.

—Glenn Gould

Musical America, 1962 Interview

Or the waterfall, or music heard so deeply
That is not heard at all, but you are the music
While the music lasts. These are only hints and guesses,
Hints followed by guesses; and the rest
Is prayer, observance, discipline, thought and action.
The hint half guessed, the gift half understood, is Incarnation.

—T. S. Elliot

"The Dry Salavages," No. 3 of Four Quartets

The longest, most arduous trip in the world is often the journey from the head to the heart. Until that round trip is completed, we remain at war with ourselves. And, of course, those at war with themselves are apt to make casualties of others, including friends and loved ones. (p. 126)

—William Sloan Coffin

Credo

Seventeen

The Gold Beneath the Shadow within Your Center

James Jordan

We are such spendthrifts with our lives. The trick of living is to slip
on and off the planet with the least of fuss you can muster. I'm not
running for sainthood. I just happen to think that in life we need
to be a little like the farmer, who puts back into the soil what he
takes out. (p. 35)

—Paul Newman

The New York Times, September 28, 2008

There are times when we must allow some of the unlived life within
us to live if we are to get new energies for living…The important
thing, as has been said before but what must be said again for
emphasis, is that we recognize the Shadow side of ourselves. This
recognition alone produces a powerful and beneficial change in
consciousness…everything in the unconscious that has been
repressed strives for reunion with consciousness. It is as though we
put certain things in the basement of our house and shut the door
tightly. But these things do not want to remain in the basement. They
turn into devils and rattle the door and seek to find some way out
of their imprisoned state and back into the world of consciousness.
In so doing they create anxiety, since we tend to fear the return
of the repressed. But this attempt of repressed contents to reach

consciousness is not simply an attempt to disturb consciousness or gain revenge. The movement is toward the light of consciousness because this is necessary if psychological redemption is to occur. No matter how malignant these split-off contents of the psyche may appear to be, and no matter how malicious their tricks, there is always the possibility of their redemption if they can reach consciousness. Paradoxically, the redemption of these lost parts of ourselves also results in our redemption. That is, we can be whole only when we have helped redeem our devils... Wholeness can only emerge when both sides of the coin are represented in consciousness at the same time; when we remain conscious of both our light and dark sides. (pp. 65, 124–25)

—Weston Noble

"Creating a Special World"

Evil: The Shadow Side of Reality by John Sanford

Man sees the things that surround him long before he becomes aware of his own self. Many of us are conscious of the hiddeness of things, but few of us sense the mystery of our own presence. (p. 61)

—Abraham Joshua Heschel

Between God and Man

Some of us get woken up by the harsh realties of life. We suffer so much that we wake up. But people keep bumping again and again into life. They still go on sleepwalking. They never wake up. Tragically, it never occurs to them that there may be a better way. Still, if **you** haven't been bumped sufficiently by life, and you haven't suffered enough, then there is another way: to **listen.** I don't mean you have to agree with what I am saying. That wouldn't be listening. Believe me, it really doesn't matter whether you agree with what I'm saying or you don't. Because agreement and disagreement have to do with words and concepts and theories. They don't have anything to do with truth. Truth is never expressed in words. Truth is sighted suddenly, as a result of a certain attitude. (pp. 16–17)

In awareness, you change, but you've got to experience it. At this point you're just taking my word for it. Perhaps also you've got a plan to become aware. Your ego, in its own cunning way, is trying to push you into awareness. Watch it! You'll meet with resistance; there will be trouble. When someone is anxious about being aware all the time, you can spot the mild anxiety. They want to be awake, to find out if they're really awake or not. That's part of **asceticism**, not awareness. (pp. 145–146)

—Anthony de Mello

Awareness

So much of what we do as artists has to do with our spirits. All authors who write on issues of the "care of the soul" attest to the importance of paying attention to matters of the soul. Better yet, they all suggest hard work, not necessarily to change or alter the inner contents of the soul, but rather to pay attention to the meanderings and journeys of the soul. Almost all authors are in agreement as to the soul's complexity as part of the human condition. Paying attention and being aware of one's soul will provide artists with the ability to be more open and potentially more vulnerable human beings.

The operative word in all matters of the soul is *awareness* of it. The simple fact that one is aware of one's inner workings provides almost immediate accessibility to all matters of the soul. The subject of this book, centering, is directly connected to matters of the soul. If one desires a center that is seated "deep within" and corresponds with the location of Center that kinesthesia and breath anchor deep within us, then "soul work" must be done almost on a daily basis.

It is helpful to imagine the soul inhabiting the same space as one's low, physical Center. For those who are unaware of the soul, it often feels as if the "soul" is at a higher location in the body. If the work has not been done to locate one's physical Center, then one can feel physically "unstable" and adrift, almost like floating in water. In this state, energy is released from the body in a random fashion, and those energies can never be channeled effectively for making music, dance, or spoken word.

In a conversation with Weston Noble as we recorded *Dialogues, Vol. 2,*[12] Weston reminded me (1) of the importance of acknowledging the aspects of our soul that Jung called "the shadow side" and (2) that acknowledgment of that shadow side is a powerful tool for placing the rest of our lives as human beings in appropriate perspective. An awareness of these "shadows" allows what Jung called "the gold beneath the shadow" to emerge in a brilliant way within us.

What we are dealing with here is in part a matter of semantics. But more importantly, it should cause an adjustment in how we think about ourselves, perceive ourselves, and most importantly affirm and love ourselves. A spiritual "core" in any artist is a powerful presence that is immediately perceivable to anyone who comes in contact with it. That "core of the soul" can be a brilliant, almost blinding inner light that can color sound, move a phrase forward, illuminate and amplify text, even move our bodies in expressive and meaningful ways. In essence, the soul is the "warm core" that Leonard

---

12 In *Dialogues, Vol. 2, The Inner Life of the Musician* (GIA, 2008), Weston Noble speaks in detail of the teachings of Carl Jung.

Bernstein talked about; it is the points of chakra energy so important in Eastern philosophy; it is the *chi* or energy center of many Eastern philosophies. Much of Center revolves around the fact that its presence within us is a result of the simple process of being awakened to the fact that we indeed possess a center. Thomas Moore, in his book *The Original Self,* speaks of the value of this type of awakening:

> It may be more important to be awake than to be successful, balanced or healthy. What does it mean to be awake? Perhaps to be living with a lively imagination, responding honestly and courageously to opportunity and avoiding the temptation to follow mere habit or collective values. It means to be an individual, in every instance manifesting the originality of who we are. This is the ultimate form of creativity—following the lead of the deep soul as we make a life.
>
> We all fall asleep and allow life to rush by without reflection and consideration. When we are shocked into awareness by tragedy or failure, this is the time not simply to make resolutions for the future, but to choose to live an awakened life. The Buddha was called "the awakened one." (pp. 126–127)
>
> —Thomas Moore
> *The Original Self*

Part of the idea behind the "gold beneath the shadow" has to do with the location within oneself of one's most deeply held beliefs and principles. Passionate beliefs seem to illuminate Center even more brilliantly, and they serve to keep one's shadow side in balance and in perspective. Beliefs are formed and solidified by much careful thought, meditation, and consideration of the important life issues. For any artist, a constant revisiting of what is important is an integral part of anchoring Center deep within oneself. As the Dalai Lama remarks in his book, *The Compassionate Life,* "My experiences are nothing special, just ordinary human ones." (p. 1) Robert Henri, in his book *The Art Spirit,* puts this matter of consideration of all things that form belief (and perhaps commitment) in the following way: "For an artist to be interesting to us he must have been interesting to himself. He must have been capable of intense feeling, and capable of profound contemplation." (p. 17)

As we consider seriously all the elements that make up Center, we do approach a "soft spot" that seems the right place for us "to be." When acknowledged, located, and sensed within, Center feels right and comfortable. Center provides a stabilizing and anchoring feeling for us as we go about not only our daily business, but our artistic business. Thomas Moore, in his book *Dark Nights of the Soul,* is quite articulate in describing this soft spot of Center: "Seriously religious people and genuine artists sometimes live out there on the outskirts of reason. They have their mystical moments and their true inspirations. They know they have to be half in this world and half in another, just to do their work. Yes, they teeter on the edge of real insanity, but generally they walk the border and have the benefits of a threshold existence." (p. 263)

For I have learned

To look on nature, not as in the hour

Of thoughtless youth; but hearing oftentimes

The still, sad music of humanity,

Nor harsh nor grating, though of ample

power

To chasten and subdue. And I have felt

A presence that disturbs me with the joy

Of elevated thoughts; a sense sublime

Of something far more deeply interfused,

Whose dwelling is the light of setting suns,

And the round ocean and the living air,

And the blue sky, and in the mind of man:

A motion and a spirit, that impels

All thinking things, all objects of all thought,

And rolls through all things. Therefore am I

still

A lover of the meadows and the woods,

And mountains; and of all that we behold

From this green earth; of all the mighty

world

Of eye, and ear,—both what they half create,

And what perceive; well pleased to

recognize

In nature and the language of the sense,

The anchor of my purest thoughts, the nurse,

The guide, the guardian of my heart, and

soul

Of all my moral being.

—William Wordsworth

Lines composed a few miles above
Tintern Abbey

Eighteen

Affirm Thyself to Know Center

James Jordan

According to Buber, the more special one is, "the more he or she has to contribute to others." … And Buber concluded, "the purer and more perfect he is, the better he knows he is a part….That is the mystery of humility." (p. 106)

—Gilya Gerda Schmidt
Martin Buber's Formative Years

Correct though Nietzsche may be for the moments when our poetic leaps are to occur, in practical living whatever is irregular or accidental can become unsettling. It forces earnest people to make their way through brambles of contradictory assignments, jumbles of duties, webs of their own making, and thickets of distraction. At such times they can be paralyzed by the awareness of how chance can produce havoc. (p. 87)

—Martin Marty and Micah Marty
When True Simplicity Is Gained

It seems to me that before a man tries to express anything to the world he must recognize in himself an individual, a new one, very distinct from others. Walt Whitman did this, and this is why I think his name so often comes to me. The one great cry of Whitman was for a man to find himself, to understand the fine thing he really is if liberated. Most people, either by training or inheritance, count themselves at the start as "no good," or "second rate" or "just like anyone else," whereas in everyone there is great mystery; every single person in the world has evidence to give of his own individuality, providing he has acquired the full power to make clear this evidence. (p. 135)

—Robert Henri
The Art Spirit

Now that we have arrived at the end of many discussions on how to enter into, access, and share Center, it is important to revisit a theme that is present throughout this book: the idea of *affirmation*.

Center cannot be accessed, stabilized, or developed without the ability to affirm one's self, artistic voice, and artistic view of the world. It is indeed easy for us to be critical of what we do. In the deep dark corners of our spirits, we constantly question whether what we are doing is artistically the "right path." The question is, where does our inability to affirm what we do as artists come from? What is evident is that this lack of ability to affirm oneself is the demon that lives within every performing artist.

Consider how affirmation is very different from ego. When we affirm ourselves in performance, the internal feeling is very different from the feeling of using the sheer force of ego to push a musical or artistic idea forward. Affirming oneself is a mindful and careful caretaking of the artistic spirit. Affirmation operates from a place of humility and great internal spaciousness that provides the proper perspective on not only the art we create, but also our sacred place within an artistic event. Affirmation requires a brilliant self-awareness and love of our deepest innermost voice, coupled with the strongest belief that our voice has some important story to tell every time we perform or, for that matter, teach.

To be in any community of artists can be a destabilizing experience. Deciding to live "within" any community of people (let alone a community of artists), without an awareness of the individual "selves" in this large community, will threaten our very ability to affirm ourselves. We can be left numb and unaware of our inner voice and inner spirit when we are swept up in the energy of larger groups of artists. In such situations we lose Center. We feel adrift in some kind of current that makes us almost unable to speak in our own voice. It is the awareness of self and awareness of Center that provide voice to the artist. Hearing one's own voice above the roar of others is most important. Hand in hand with the ability to affirm oneself as an artist is the ability to maintain this very real sense of self.

Great teachers affirm every day of their lives. They also happen to teach. While they teach, they constantly affirm a student's worth. In fact, teaching is a by-product of the affirmation of others in the teaching process. And self affirmation is the only sure route to honest artististic expression. By being able to affirm him or herself devoid of ego, the artist allows the artistic voice to speak clearly through the sound of the voice or the movement of the body. Movement and sound are borne out of a Center that is anchored and stabilized through affirmation of self and hum and musical self-worth. We artists will also find that the affirmed place within us lives in the same place as our physical Center, and that when we are truly in that place, our "focus" is both vibrant and brilliant. Another definition for affirmation would be: the ability to face oneself with great love and care.

There must be, above all, an ability to cherish oneself, one's voice, and one's ideas. Additionally, one must also be able to extend that affirmation to others in their everyday artistic interactions. Artists must also realize that by working within communities of artists, they may be more easily able to affirm their self-worth. The danger in such encounters is that one loses one's sense of Center because of, at times, the seemingly overpowering energy of many. The paradox is that the voice of such groups can only be as strong as the centered voices that occupy that group.

In closing the ideas of this book, consider what a powerful role affirmation of self and affirmation of others play in an artist's life that is centered, grounded, and focused. As expressed at the beginning of this book, centering is the most powerful artistic tool in the teaching process. The ability to find Center, has organized many a chaotic rehearsal or performance. And when able to operate from that deeply internal and spacious place, I am deeply humbled about what a life in the creative arts can do for not only ourselves but for others.

Affirmation of self goes far beyond what is commonly referred to as a "healthy self image." Such concepts of self-image seem to be mostly external events that avoid inner exploration of one's Center. And while love of self is an important part of any artist's life, the word "affirmation" should signal a broader perspective on what it is to believe that what we have to offer to the artistic world is worthwhile.

Nineteen
The Crossing Point

James Jordan

Nature and God—I neither knew
Yet Both so well knew me
They startled, like Executors
Of My Identity.

—Emily Dickinson

Poem 835, Excerpt Complete Poems of Emily Dickinson

To behold with awe is to see things filled with their own light, their own Bit of Being, and to be moved by a sense of the numinous.[13] This light and this bit of being are gifts of creation. As gifts, they fill us with awe. This awe is accompanied by delight. It is the original blessing. (p. 140)

—Mary Caroline Richards

Opening Our Moral Eye

---

13   Numinous/nyoominss/adjective having a strong religious or spiritual quality. ORIGIN from Latin numen. Oxford English Dictionary.

CENTERING, which I discuss in this book, is a severe and thrilling discipline, often acutely unpleasant. In my own efforts, I become weak, discouraged, exhausted, angry, frustrated, unhappy, and confused. But someone within me is resolute, and I try again. Within us lives a merciful being who helps us to our feet however many times we fall. (p. 8)

—Mary Caroline Richards

Centering

"I'm afraid I don't understand anything more at all," I answered, "even the simplest things have got in a muddle. Is it 'I' who draw the bow, or is it the bow that draws me into the state of highest tension? Do 'I' hit the goal, or does the goal hit me? Is 'It' spiritual when seen by the eyes of the body, and corporeal when seen by the eyes of the spirit—or both or neither? Bow, arrow, goal and ego, all melt into one another, so that I can no longer separate them. And even the need to separate has gone. For as soon as I take the bow and shoot, everything becomes so clear and straightforward and so ridiculously simple…."

"Now at last," the Master broke in, "the bowstring has cut right through you." (p. 61)

—Eugen Herrigel

Zen in the Art of Archery

Dann man gerade nur denkt, das worüber man denkt, man gar nicht ausdenken kann.

(Then only are we really thinking when the subject on which we are thinking cannot be thought out.)

—Goethe

Centering by M. C. Richards (Epigraph)

I sense things that have happened to me as somehow characteristic of the human lot, transcending personality, bearing within them a form which can reveal to my consciousness and to others deeper meanings than those of private sensation. I sense structures everywhere at work, in realms to which sensations lead us but where they change into insight and compassion. The deeper we go into these realms, the more contact we make with another's reality. The sharper the sense of pain and bliss as they interweave through the heartbreak and luck of life, the more the line between self and other may dissolve. It is a physique–soul–alchemy: a transformation of inner and outer. (p. 4)

—Mary Caroline Richards

Centering

Look, the pureness of sound that should be here is like a child's love, like a child's smile, tender, not mature. But it's powerful. It lights up the whole place. Just that countenance is what you should hear here. (p. 31)

—Frank Battisti

Diane Asseo Griliches

The artist's life cannot be otherwise than full of conflicts, for two forces are at war within him—on one hand the common human longing for happiness, satisfaction and security in life, and on the other, a ruthless passion for creation which may go so far as to override every personal desire….There are hardly any exceptions to the rule that a person must pay dearly for the divine gift of creative fire.

—Carl Jung

Free Play by Stephen Nachmanovich

The connections which I want particularly to celebrate here today are those between the inner invisible realm of the "force" and the outer visible realm of the "flower," the inner realm of nature and the inner realm of man, connections between the invisible life of man and the invisible life of the universe, invisible that is to ordinary eyesight. Connections between human beings, between fields of study and work, the fabric of a common spiritual community. Artists are sometimes particularly attuned to these connections, scientists too, mystics too, soul-brothers too. (p. 171)

—M. C. Richards

The Crossing Point

M. C. Richards

There are no coincidences in life, and there are certainly no coincidences in an artist's life. Things seem to happen for a particular reason at a particular time as long as we are open to both the events and the suggestions that those events have for our lives. This book began as a relatively naïve journey to document things I have learned about Center and to bring to a wider audience the work of M. C. Richards and others concerning this powerful concept. As Nova and I talked and wrote, I became fascinated with the many roads one could take to begin to understand not only what Center "is" but how Center "happens."

Serendipity also plays a role many times in our creative lives. In the process of moving this volume through editing, my editor on this book, Edith Bicknell, brought to my attention a film she had seen in Maine on M. C. Richards! I was stunned that such a thing existed and immediately got a copy of *The Fire Within* and *Creativity* produced by renowned director Arthur Penn. For me, and hopefully for you, these films have illuminated and provided the "missing links" in my understanding of Center as seen through the incredible genius of this unsung hero of all those artistic, M. C. Richards. Her journey toward Center, coupled with a real sense of what it is to not only be centered but also authentic, provided intellectual clarity and artistic clarity for me and, as it has happened, provides a type of closure for all the ideas presented in this book for your thought and consideration.

One thing that is ever so clear now is that without Center, there can be little authentic and artistic communication by an artist, regardless of medium. Whether it be the actor on the stage, the dancer, the classroom music teacher, or the conductor, a profound understanding of what it is to be centered, with all its complexities, must be central to any artistic endeavor. It is as important for the development of a conductor as it is for a singer, actor, dancer, and even a teacher of any of the arts. One cannot guide another on a journey that one has not taken oneself. What follows is an attempt to summarize the ideas of M. C. Richards as observed on *The Fire Within* and to make connections into our lives and our musicing, acting, dancing, and speaking.

There is another startling revelation that has come out of this serendipity. Much of what I have come to understand as an artist is profoundly rooted in the ideas of M. C. Richards. I now realize that my teacher, Elaine Brown, understood these basic beliefs about authenticity: the "source," the crossing point, and the privilege of being with other artists. Acting as a muse and mystic (M. C. Richards always said that people who know their Center are both clairvoyants and mystics), Elaine Brown melded the ideas of M. C. Richards and Martin Buber to arrive at her very clear and crystalline sense of Center. And she taught M. C. Richards and Buber through her own crossing point. It is apparent that the writings of M. C. Richards had a profound effect upon all that Elaine Brown did and lived; and Elaine mystically transferred to us, her students, that awe for the creative process of musicing and teaching. Elaine's art was her life and her life was her art, and this anchored all the disparate elements of Center within us. As M. C. Richards says in the video, *The Fire Within,* "Do not leave your heart in the studio."

M. C. Richards said that in the end, "Centering is the discipline of bringing in rather than leaving out."[14] What we have tried to do in this book, unknowingly at first, is to bring into our awareness as artists all of the components that make up our Center. After over thirty years of hearing this material, for the first time it is clear that Center and all its components not only make the artist but also generate artistry and creativity. Center must

---

14   M. C Richards, *Opening Our Moral Eye*, p. 70.

be both the starting and ending points in our self-education as artists and teachers. It is the way, as M. C. Richards so elegantly states, "We author our lives."

A Brief Biography

The story of the life of M. C. Richards and her achievements needs to be known to the greater artistic world. She received a Ph.D. from the University of California at Berkeley in 1942 and accepted a tenure-track position at the University of Chicago. Disillusioned with academia, she left the University of Chicago for Black Mountain College in North Carolina.[15] For little money, and probably less job security, she went to a place where creativity and the creative act were respected and where freedom for creativity was allowed. Because of that freedom, Black Mountain attracted this remarkable group of artists and thinkers: Robert Turner, Josef Albers, Louis Harrison, Stefan Wolpe, Willem DeKooning, Robert Rauschenberg, John Cage, Merce Cunningham, Buckminster Fuller, Karen Karnes, and Charles Olsen. In a sense, it was America's artistic Mecca. With M. C. Richards as chair of the faculty, these innovators taught and created collaborative performances at Black Mountain.

In the summer of 1952 the institution also experienced a seismic event in the music world: John Cage's *First Happening*. Parallel with this musical event came a monumental event in the history of theater, M. C. Richards'

---

15   Martin Duberman wrote an in-depth historical study of the life and death of Black Mountain College in *Black Mountain: An Exploration in Community*. The book documents the institution's struggles and triumphs, and its impact upon creative life in America.

translation of Antonin Artaud's *The Theater and Its Double.* The change caused in American theater was almost instantaneous. In *The Fire Within,* Judith Malena commented on this event:

> M. C. made us, through Artaud, to understand theater in a white new light. To find the truth, insist on the truth, never make a fake gesture, never do anything false, because it is a betrayal of your life and your work. You couldn't do that anymore after M. C's translation of Artaud; you have to be for real.

Black Mountain College closed in 1956, but its deep mark upon American creative life had been made. Despite successes and travails, the people at Black Mountain demonstrated not only artistic curiosity but also artistic guts and courage. M. C. Richards then created an artistic commune at Stony Point in New York and closed out her life by working in Camphill Village, an alternative educational community based on the teachings of Rudolph Steiner. She passed away September 10, 1999.

When Will "IT" Happen?

You cannot make Center by simply willing it to happen. Center happens over a long period of gestation composed of intense thought, study, and eventual understandings. Once they understand what composes Center, most artists want to go about the process of acquiring it quickly! M. C. Richards tells the following story:

Once in a dream I was standing in my vegetable garden. Fifty feet away, on the compost pile stood a Being smiling strangely. It had three eyes. The right eye was a sun, the middle eye was a diamond and the left was a human eye but huge, as huge as the diamond and the sun. The being had a benign expression on its countenance….

In my dream I found myself asking the Being a question, a kind of question one might ask the I Ching book of oracles. The question began: "When will I…when will my time…what is my destiny?"… It was a question in a question.

The Being, who seemed to be from the daimonic realm, answered, "I wouldn't worry about that if I were you." (p. 19)

—M. C. Richards

Opening Our Moral Eye

"The Dream" by M. C. Richards.

It can be safely said that acquiring Center requires an extended gestation period—time for one to stay in awareness to contemplate all the elements that compose one's Center. M. C. Richards tells us that the major challenge of moving toward Center is tapping into our own silences with a sharpened ability to listen to ourselves, a receptivity to hear the vast number of inaudibles within that are, until we make ourselves aware, truly components of Center we will never "hear."[16]

Centering Is the Discipline of Bringing In Rather than Leaving Out

Imagination is spiritual perception. Authenticity is spiritual presence. In reflecting on the theme of this talk, authenticity and imagination appeared in my inner eye, as companions. We can think of authenticity as the quality of expression, and imagination appears as the realm of Source, what authenticity draws upon. Or the other way around: authenticity gives impulse, imagination gives us the image. We need the courage of authenticity to carry the originality of imagination into expression. Whichever way you want to figure it, imagination and authenticity are double doors to creation. (p. 118)

—M. C. Richards

Opening Our Moral Eye

---

16   This concept of hearing the inaudible as a path to Center is described by Richards in all of her books, and specifically in the film, *The Fire Within.*

Most musicians want to make "honest" music. Actors want to be honest on stage, as do dancers. Honesty is mentioned as a catchall that somehow must be in every performance. Many of us believe that this honesty is created "in the moment" when, in reality, honesty or authenticity is a direct product of our individual spiritual content. One isn't simply honest; one is honest in one's way of being with others.

Many years ago upon coming to Westminster Choir College, when I asked how my work would be judged I was told that it would be judged by the honesty of its content. That simple phrase set me on an exploration for a definition of "honesty" in performance—and finding a clear definition that employs specifics has proved troublesome. The answer was not easy, nor was it forthcoming. And it was not until recent years that I realized that the "honesty" thing was tied and intimately connected to my own spirituality.

Talking of spirituality is indeed a slippery slope for artists. In *The Musician's Soul*, I attempted to define the lines between one's spirituality and one's religiosity. As many of us would agree, our spirituality as artists goes beyond our own particular religiosity. Many of us believe that if we are spiritual beings, spirituality will somehow make its way into our art. But *wanting to be* spiritual and actually operating from or within a spiritual place are two very different artistic perspectives.

M. C. Richards' stupendously simple revelation, "Imagination is spiritual perception. Authenticity is spiritual presence," clarifies not only a definition of spirituality for an artist, but how to acquire that "spiritual perception"—that is, how to make one's spirituality a living, vibrant, almost mystical presence in one's art. Spirituality and honesty are one in the same. M. C. Richards wrote that authenticity and imagination are "companions."

But the most important distinction for M. C. Richards was what she referred to as "the Source." It is "the Source" from which authenticity is drawn. As she so elegantly stated, "Whichever way you want to figure it, imagination and authenticity are the double-doors to creation."[17] In her world (and ours), authenticity doesn't just happen; it must be developed. That authenticity, when developed, can only speak through a centered person and human soul fed by "the Source" that provides our mystical direction. Authenticity is very much an important component of one's many-faceted Center as an artist.

> Authenticity may seem bold, for it's often original, one of a kind. Separate from consensus. One comes to it through trust in one's own self, and a willingness to entrust oneself to others, whatever the risk. Vulnerability at some point dissolves into stillness. This stillness can act, and does act, for children and the child in oneself, as a kind of buffer, an insulating protection, which allows one to be authentic and at risk in a natural way. (p. 120)

> —M. C. Richards
> *Opening Our Moral Eye*

Artists Live in the "Crossing Point"

> The plant has two forces. The part that goes up into the light and the force that goes into the dark, into the earth. There is a place in some plants that is only one cell wide called "the crossing point"— where those two impulses co-exist. This is where our wholeness is.

> —M. C. Richards
> *The Fire Within*

---

17   M. C. Richards, *Opening Our Moral Eye*, p. 118.

Discussed earlier in this book, there is a duality of being an artist and the challenges that artistic path brings. However, there hasn't been a clear paradigm for allowing the artistic opposites within oneself to harmoniously co-exist. For a period of my creative life, it felt so much better (and easier) to just do one rather than keep the two in perspective and balance. I could be in a spiritual place *or* a grounded place. But is it is now very clear (thank you, M. C. Richards!) that being truly centered requires us *to be* and *to live* in this mystical "crossing point." This is the point in us where our desire for human connection to others is counterbalanced by a rootedness firmly established in what we believe to be so—a "force,"[18] as M. C. Richards states, that goes up into the light and down into the ground; a love for others and an affirmation to love oneself; an ability to use breath to open Center to others and to ourselves; the ability to move between hard focus and soft focus; the ability to understand and perceive our circles of attention; the ability to deeply understand where all these opposite impulses exist *harmoniously* within us.

A vivid image appears when we visualize our Center as a *crossing point* within us—when our anatomical and structural Center resides in the very same place as our need for authenticity and honesty. When that place is intimately understood after careful thought and inward silence, we will each arrive at an artistic/spiritual place where we engage the art we love at every turn. We must have the courage to pursue the difficult type of artistic exploration that is never afraid to take a chance with either an artistic idea or a human one. As M. C. Richards stated so elegantly, "Centering is the discipline of bringing in rather than leaving out."[19] We should not worry about how long

---

18   All of the references in quotes from M. C. Richards are taken from the film, *The Fire Within.*
19   M. C. Richards, *Opening Our Moral Eye*, p. 70.

it will take to understand Center, for the understanding of Center is our journey as artists, and understanding has a way of taking care of itself and us. Center is beyond mundane technique, but gives understanding of the simplicity of artistic expression. "Hang in for the journey," M. C. Richards would say. Pick yourself up when you stumble or don't quite understand. Keep listening to yourself and the world. The "crossing point" (also known as Center) will be a place where you will find your most inspiring and awe-creating artistic expression. To do so will be to unleash a creative spirit that will always be authentic, honest, and humanly compelling.

> Every artist copes with reality by means of his fantasy. Fantasy, better known as imagination, is his greatest treasure, his basic equipment for life. And since his work is his life, his fantasy is constantly in play. He dreams life. Psychologists tell us that a child's imagination reaches its peak at the age of six or seven, then is gradually inhibited, diminished to conform with the attitudes of his elders—that is, reality. Alas. Perhaps what distinguishes artists from regular folks is that for whatever reasons, their imaginative drive is less inhibited; they have retained in adulthood more of that five-year-old's fantasy than others have. This is not to say that an artist is the childlike madman the old romantic traditions have made him out to be; he is usually capable of brushing his teeth, keeping track of his love life, or counting his change in a taxicab. When I speak of his *fantasy* I am not suggesting a constant state of abstraction, but rather the continuous imaginative powers that inform his creative acts as well as his reactions to the world around him. And out of that creativity, and those imaginative reactions come not idle dreams, but truths—all those abiding truth formations and constellations that nourish us, from Dante to Joyce, from Bach to the Beatles, from Praxiteles to Picasso. (pp. 358–359)
>
> —Leonard Bernstein
> *Findings*

Conclusions

This book has brought full circle many concepts I have discussed in previous books, especially *The Musician's Soul, The Musician's Spirit,* and *The Musician's Walk.* But it is now very clear to me that the major inspiration in my creative life, Elaine Brown, understood M. C. Richards' work intimately. As I carefully read and re-read M. C. Richards' book *Centering,* I come across phrases or concepts that I vividly recall Elaine saying. *Centering* was *the* first book Elaine Brown assigned us all to read. It was the book she and I discussed in lessons. She always said to me, "You may not understand this now, but you will years from now." Elaine was my musical mystic. It is clear now that M. C. Richards' book illuminated her pathway. That is not in any way to minimize Elaine's communicative and human gifts. She was the most centered person I ever knew, and I now know that I learned centering through osmosis! Many of you reading this book will have had persons in your development as artists who did the same for you. The common thread, no matter what they called it, is for all of us to find our voice, our own Center, through which our authenticity is born. No matter your musical or creative path, as performer or teacher, consider the power of your own Center and be brave enough to live in your own "crossing point."

Recommended Resources

Duberman, Martin. *Black Mountain: An Exploration in Community.*
Evanston, IL: Northwestern University Press, 1972.

Moore, Thomas. *Care of the Soul.* New York: HarperCollins Publishers,
1992.

Nachmanovitch, Stephen. *Free Play: Improvisation in Life and Art.* New
York: Penguin Putnam, Inc., 1990.

Richards, M. C. *The Crossing Point: Selected Talks and Writings.* London:
Wesleyan University Press, 1973.

Richards, M. C. *Opening Our Moral Eye: Essays, Talks and Poems
Embracing Creativity and Community.* Hudson, New York:
Lindisfarne Press, 1996.

NOTE: For anyone reading this book, the viewing of the following
inspirational DVDs is not only encouraged but highly recommended.
The journeys on these DVDs not only document the deeply held
ideas of M. C. Richards but also guide one gently and carefully
through the profound ideas that contribute to one's life as an artist
in this world. Ideas presented on these DVDs move the viewer
closer to a definition of Center, authenticity, and spiritual presence,
and their roles in honest artistic creation.

Penn, Arthur. *Creativity: Clay, Color and Word—An M. C. Richards
Workshop.* Kane-Lewis Productions, 2006.www.mcrichardsfilms.
com.

Richards, M. C. *The Fire Within.* Kane-Lewis Productions, 2003. www.
mcrichardsfilms.com.

Twenty
Meditations Before Performing or Teaching

James Jordan

Note:
This chapter is a collection of quotes
that may be helpful to artists for reconnecting with Center.

Or the waterfall, or music heard so deeply
That is not heard at all, but you are the music
While the music lasts. These are only hints and guesses,
Hints followed by guesses; and the rest
Is prayer, observance, discipline, thought and action.
The hint half guessed, the gift half understood, is Incarnation.

—T. S. Elliot

"The Dry Salavages" No. 3 of Four Quartets

…Blunt the sharpness.
Untangle the knot,
Soften the glare,
Merge with Dust.

—Lao Tzu
Tao Te Ching: Four

We grow accustomed to the Dark—
When light is put away—
And when the Neighbor holds the Lamp
To witness her Goodbye—

A Moment—We uncertain step
For newness of the night—
Then—fit our Vision to the Dark—
And meet the Road—erect—

And so of larger—Darkness—
Those Evenings of the Brain—
When not a Moon disclose a sign—
Or star—come out—within—

The Bravest—grope a little—
And sometimes hit a Tree
Directly in the Forehead—
But as they learn to see—

Either the Darkness alters—
Or something in the sight
Adjusts itself to Midnight—
And Life steps almost straight.

—Emily Dickinson

Hear, and your Soul shall live.

—Isaiah 55:3

In every artist's development the germ of the later work is always found in the earlier. The nucleus around which the artist's intellect builds his work is himself…and this changes little from birth to death.

The only real influence I've ever had was myself. (p xii)

—Edward Hopper

The Soul's Code by James Hillman

The purpose of art is not the release of a momentary ejection of adrenalin, but is, rather, the gradual, lifelong construction of a state of wonder and serenity.

—Glenn Gould

Musical America, Interview 1962

We lose too much of essential qualities in the civilizing process. We are a web of inhibitions… And a musician must be one to whom something is more important than himself.

One of the most beautiful stories I know concerns a certain African tribe in which, at the time when the boy passes into manhood he must go off into the jungle by himself—there to indulge in an orgy of dancing and shouting and wailing and sobbing. He must leave the village—for his sounds would make the people in the village ill.

Kathleen Ferriers and Eileen Farrells and Toscaninis and Walters are great because they find the basic and, finally, simple human sound in what for the rest of us are mazes of complexity. (p. 346)

—Robert Shaw

The Robert Shaw Reader by Robert Blocker

What a wonderful thing it would be if once and for all we could lay to rest the notion that it is a virtue to love others and a vice to love oneself. For what is vicious is not self-love but selfishness, and selfishness is more a product of self-hate, than self love. All forms of selfishness are finally forms of insecurity, compensations for the lack of self-love. (p. 21)

—William Sloan Coffin

Credo

Always the wish that you may find patience enough in yourself to endure, and simplicity enough to believe; that you may acquire more and more confidence in that which is difficult, and in your solitude among others. (p. 120)

—Rainer Maria Rilke

Walking in This World by Julia Cameron

Know that you are both intelligent and stupid, often in the same moment. Admit to what you desire and what you fear. If you did little more than these two things, you would be filled with irony and your actions would be infinitely more trustworthy for their honesty. It's all right to have grand and eccentric longings. It's all right to be afraid. Only by embracing these two emotional pillars will you glimpse the nature of your soul, which is the ground of your existence. (p. 114)

—Thomas Moore

Dark Nights of the Soul

There are times when we must allow some of the unlived life within us to live if we are to get new energies for living. The important thing, as has been said before but what must be said again for emphasis, is that we recognize the Shadow side of ourselves. This recognition alone produces a powerful and beneficial change in consciousness.... Everything in the unconscious that has been repressed strives for reunion with consciousness. It is as though we put certain things in the basement of our house and shut the door tightly. But these things do not want to remain in the basement. They turn into devils and rattle the door and seek to find some way out of their imprisoned state and back into the world of consciousness. In so doing they create anxiety, since we tend to fear the return of the repressed. But this attempt of repressed contents to reach consciousness is not simply an attempt to disturb consciousness or gain revenge. The movement is toward the light of consciousness because this is necessary if psychological redemption is to occur. No matter how malignant these split-off contents of the psyche may appear to be, and no matter how malicious their tricks, there is always the possibility of their redemption if they can reach consciousness. Paradoxically, the redemption of these lost parts of ourselves also results in our redemption. That is, we can be whole only when we have helped redeem our devils....Wholeness can only emerge when both sides of the coin are represented in consciousness at the same time; when we remain conscious of both our light and dark sides. (p. 65, pp. 124–125)

—Weston Noble

"Creating a Special World"

Evil: The Shadow Side of Reality by John Sanford

Man achieves fullness of being in fellowship, in care for others. He expands his existence by "bearing his fellow-man's burden." As we have said, animals are concerned for their own needs; the degree of our being human stands in direct proportion to the degree in which we care for others. (p. 47)

The sense of wonder is not the mist in our eyes or the fog in our words. Wonder or radical amazement, is a way of going beyond what is given in thing and thought, refusing to take anything for granted, to regard anything as final. It is our honest response to the grandeur and mystery of reality, our confrontation with that which transcends the given. (p. 79)

—Abraham Joshua Heschel

Who Is Man?

People say that what we're all seeking is a meaning for life. I don't think that's what we're really seeking. I think that what we are seeking is an experience of being alive, so that our life experiences on the purely physical plane will have resonances with our innermost being and reality, so that we actually feel the rapture of being alive. That's what its finally about. (p. 5)

—Joseph Campbell

The Power of Myth

The relationships between performers and their instruments and performers and their audiences can create a dilemma. This aspect of a performer's presence in front of their audience is often neglected in lessons due to emphasis on what is perceived to be basic technique. What I have found is that unless the lesson includes work on presence, as much as 40 percent of tone quality can be missing. (p. 848)

The first prerequisite for presence in performance is focusing on the musical message rather than yourself. Often I have to remind students that the message is far more important than the performer. The passion and enthusiasm of the music must be fueled by a genuine desire of the performer to be there. (p. 851)

—Meribeth Bunch

"Are you all there?"

The Strad, August 2002

Bibliography

Abernethy, Bob, and Williams Bole. *The Life of Meaning.* New York: Seven Stories Press, 2007.

Arneson, Christopher, Keith Buhl, and Nova Thomas. *Voice and Speech for the Stanislavsky Actor: A Curriculum Manual for Teachers.* Actors Studio Drama School, New School University, 2004.

Aitken, Robert. *The Morning Star: New and Selected Writings.* Honolulu, HI: Shoemaker and Hoard, 2003.

Austin, Jmes J. *Zen and the Brain: Toward an Understanding of Meditation and Consciousness.* Cambridge, MA: MIT Press, 1998.

Barenboim, Daniel. *Music Quickens Time.* London: Verso. 2008.

Bernstein Leonard. *Findings.* New York: Doubleday, 1982.

———. *The Joy of Music.* New York. Simon and Schuster, 1959.

Blocker, Robert, ed. *The Robert Shaw Reader.* New Haven, CT: Yale University Press, 2004.

Bono. "Notes from the Chairman." *The New York Times,* January 11, 2009.

Brenen, F. "The Relation Between Musical Capacity and Performance." *Psychological Review* 36 (1926): 249–62.

Brubach, Holly. "A Pianist for Whom Never Was Never an Option." *The New York Times,* June 10, 2007, pp. 25–7.

Buber, Martin. *Between Man and Man.* New York: Collier Books, 1965.

———. *I and Thou.* New York: Macmillan, 1958.

Bunch, Meribeth. "Are You All There?" *The Strad,* August 2002, pp. 848–52.

Campbell, Don G. *Master Teacher: Nadia Boulanger.* Washington, DC: The Pastoral Press, 1984.

Campbell, Joseph. *The Power of Myth.* New York: Doubleday, 1988.

Carlson, Janet. *Quick, Before the Music Stops: How Ballroom Dancing Saved My Life.* New York: Broadway Books, 2008.

Carnicke, Sharon M. *Stanislavsky in Focus.* London and New York: Routledge, 1998.

Chekhov, Michael. *To the Actor, On the Technique of Acting.* New York: Harper and Row, 1969.

Coffin, William Sloane. *Credo.* Louisville, KY: Westminster John Knox Press, 2004.

Copland, Aaron. *Music and Imagination.* New York: New American Library, 1952.

DeMello, Anthony. *Awareness: The Perils and Opportunities of Reality.* New York: Doubleday, 1990.

Dewey, John. *Experience and Education.* New York: Simon and Schuster, 1938.

Dowrick, Stephanie. *Intimacy and Solitude: Balancing Closeness and Independence.* New York: W. W. Norton, 1991.

Duberman, Martin. *Black Mountain: An Exploration in Community.* Evanston: Northwestern University Press, 1972.

Ekman, Paul, ed. *Emotional Awareness: A Conversation between The Dalai Lama and Paul Ekman, Ph.D.* New York: Henry Holt and Company, 2008.

Emerson, Ralph Waldo. *Essays and English Traits, Vol. V.* Accessed bartleby.com.

Epstein, Mark. *Psychotherapy without the Self: A Buddhist Perspective.* New Haven, CT: Yale University Press, 2007.

Gardner, Howard. *Frames of Mind.* New York: Basic Books, 1983.

Gelb, Michael. *Body Learning.* New York: Henry Holt and Company, 1987.

Goleman, Tara-Bennett. *Emotional Alchemy.* New York: Three Rivers Press, 2001.

Greene, Don, Ph.D. *Performance Success: Performing Your Best Under Pressure.* New York and London: Routledge, 2002.

Griliches, Dine Asseo. *Teaching Musicians: A Photographer's View.* Piermont, NH: Bunker Hill Publishing, 2008.

Hackney, Peggy. *Making Connections: Total Body Integration through Bartenieff Fundamentals.* New York: Routledge, 2002.

Hanna, Thomas. *The Body of Life: Creating New Pathways for Sensory Awareness and Fluid Movement.* Rochester, VT: Healing Arts Press, 1993.

Hartley, Linda. *Somatic Psychology: Body, Mind and Meaning.* Philadelphia, PA: Whurr Publishers, 2004.

Henri, Robert. *The Art Spirit.* Boulder, CO: Westview Press, 1984. Originally published in 1923.

Heschel, Abraham Joshua. *I Asked for Wonder.* New York: Crossroad Press, 1998.

Highwater, Jamake. *The Primal Mind.* New York: Meridian, 1981.

Hillman, James. *Anima: An Anatomy of a Personified Notion.* Putnam, CT: Spring Publications, Inc., 2007.

———. *Re-Visioning Psychology.* New York: Harper Perennial Publishers, 1992.

———. *The Thought of the Heart and the Soul of the World.* Dallas, TX: Spring Publications, 1982.

Huther, Gerald. *The Compassionate Brain.* Boston, MA: Trumpeter, 2006.

Jordan, James. *The Musician's Soul.* Chicago: GIA Publications, Inc., 1999.

Kabat-Zin, Jon. *Wherever You Go There You Are.* New York: Hyperion Books, 1994.

Kaplan, Edward K. *Spiritual Radical: Abraham Joshua Heschel in America.* New Haven, CT: Yale University Press, 2007.

Laban, Rudolf von. *A Life for Dance.* London: MacDonald and Evans, Ltd., 1975.

———. "Movement Concerns the Whole Man." *The Laban Art of Movement Build Magazine* 21 (November 1958): pp. 12–3.

Laban, Rudolf von, and F. C. Lawrence. *Effort.* London: MacDonald and Evans, Ltd., 947.

Laban, Rudolf von. Lisa Ullman, ed. *Choreutics.* London: MacDonald and Evans, Ltd., 1966.

———. *Modern Educational Dance.* Boston, MA: Plays, Inc., 1980.

Lamb, Warren. *Posture and Gesture.* London: Gerald Duckworth and Company, 1965.

Marty, Martin, and Micah Marty. *When True Simplicity Is Gained: Finding Spiritual Clarity in a Complex World.* Cambridge: Wm. B. Eerdmans, 1998.

May, Gerald G. *Will and Spirit.* San Francisco, CA: Harper, 1987.

Merlin, Bella. *The Complete Stanislavsky Toolkit.* Hollywood, CA: Drama Publishers, Quite Specific Media Group, Ltd., 2007.

Moore, Thomas. *Care of the Soul.* New York: HarperCollins Publishers, 1994.

Nachmanovitch, Stephen. *Free Play: Improvisation in Life and Art.* New York: Penguin Putnam, Inc., 1990.

O'Shaughnessy, Ann, and Roderick MacIver. *Art as a Way of Life.* North Ferrisburg, VT: Herron Dance Press, 2006.

Ponce, Charles. *Working of the Soul: Reflections on Jungian Psychology.* Berkeley: North Atlantic Books, 1988.

Richards, Mary Caroline. *Centering.* Middletown, CT: Wesleyan University Press, 1989.

————. *Opening Our Moral Eye: Essays, Talks and Poems Embracing Creativity and Community.* Hudson, New York: Lindisfarne Press, 1996.

————. *The Crossing Point.* Middletown, CT: Wesleyan University Press, 1973.

Schmidt, Gilya Gerda. *Martin Buber's Formative Years.* London: University of Alabama Press, 1995.

Seo. Audrey Yoshiko. *Enso: Zen Circles of Enlightenment.* Boston, MA: Wetherhill, 2007.

Storr, Anthony. *Music and the Mind.* New York: Ballantine Books, 1992.

————. *Solitude. A Return to the Self.* New York: Ballantine Books, 1988.

Swafford, Jan. *Johannes Brahms: A Biography.* New York: Random House, 1999.

Vasileios, Archimandrite. *Abba Isaac the Syrian: An Approach to His World.* Montreal: Alexander Press, 1997.

Wehr, David A. "John Finley Williamson (1887–1964): His Life and Contribution to Choral Music." Ph.D. diss., University of Miami, 1971. University Microfilms 72–12, 878.

NOTE: For anyone reading this book, the viewing of the following inspirational DVDs is not only encouraged but highly recommended. The journeys on these DVDs not only document the deeply held ideas of M. C. Richards but also guide one gently and carefully through the profound ideas that contribute to one's life as an artist in this world. Ideas presented on these DVDs move the viewer closer to a definition of Center, authenticity, and spiritual presence, and their roles in honest artistic creation.

Penn, Arthur. *Creativity: Clay, Color and Word—An M. C. Richards Workshop*. Kane-Lewis Productions, 2006. www.mcrichardsfilms. com.

Richards, M. C. *The Fire Within*. Kane-Lewis Productions, 2003. www. mcrichardsfilms.com.

About the Authors

James Jordan

James Jordan is considered to be one of the most influential choral conductors and educators in America. His more than eighteen books covering rehearsal and teaching pedagogy, conducting technique, and the spirituality of musicing, as well as numerous DVDs and recordings, have brought about far-reaching pedagogical and philosophical changes not only in choral music but also in the worlds of orchestral conducting, wind conducting, piano, and music education. The Choral Journal has described his writings as "visionary." Renowned American composer Morten Lauridsen dedicated the third movement of his Midwinter Songs to him.

One of the country's leading choral artists, Dr. Jordan is Senior Conductor at Westminster Choir College of Rider University, where he conducts the Westminster Williamson Voices and the Westminster Schola Cantorum, and teaches undergraduate and graduate choral conducting. Over thirty works have been premiered by the Westminster Williamson Voices, including the works of Mantyjaarvi, Custer, Ames, Hill, Whitbourn, Henson, and Wilberg. Dr. Jordan also conducts Anam Cara (www.anamcarachoir.com), a professional choral ensemble based in Philadelphia that has received critical acclaim for its recordings. The American Record Review wrote that Anam Cara "is a choir to please the fussiest choral connoisseur" and called their inaugural recording, Innisfree, "skillful and shining," "glowing," "supremely accomplished" with a "tone that produces a wide range of effects from vocal transparency to rich, full-throated glory."

Dr. Jordan is one of the country's most prolific writers on the subjects of the philosophy of music making and choral teaching. His trilogy of books on the philosophy and spirituality of musicing—The Musician's Soul, The Musician's Spirit, and The Musician's Walk—have made a deep and profound impact upon musicians and teachers around the world. Dr. Jordan is also Executive Editor of the Evoking Sound Choral Series (GIA), which now includes over one hundred published works. In addition, he delivers over thirty workshops and keynote addresses each year in addition to an extensive conducting schedule.

Dr. Jordan has had the unique privilege of studying with several of the landmark teachers of the twentieth century. He was a student of Elaine Brown, Wilhelm Ehmann, and Frauke Haasemann. He completed his Ph.D. in Psychology of Music under Edwin Gordon. He has been the recipient of many awards for his contributions to the profession. He was named Distinguished Choral Scholar at The University of Alberta. He was made an honorary member of Phi Mu Alpha Sinfonia in 2002 at Florida State University.

Dr. Jordan's lecture/teaching schedule and writings are detailed on his Web site (www.evokingsound.com) and his publisher's Web site (www.giamusic.com/jordan).

Nova Thomas

Nova Thomas is an Assistant Professor of Voice at Westminster Choir College of Rider University and Director of the university's Music Theater Program. Her teaching responsibilities include private vocal instruction (for both graduate and undergraduate students), dramatic coaching and role preparation, four progressive semesters of classes for the singing-actor, and a special topics course in Bel Canto. Additionally, she is in much demand as a master class teacher and speaker. Recent engagements in this capacity include classes and lectures with the National Association of Teachers of Singing (NATS) and National Opera Association Winter Conference, an OPERA America-sponsored event on the training of big voices, a master class with the Florence Voice Seminar, and several university master classes.

Ms. Thomas is also a teaching-artist and dramatic coach for Westminster Choir College's CoOPERAtive program, a master teacher for the Conducting Institute, and co-teacher with renowned actor and TONY award winner Denis O'Hare for the Summer Music Theater Immersion Experience in New York City. Other academic appointments include Professor of Professional Practice and Voice and Speech Departmental Chair at the New School for Drama, New School University (formerly the Actors Studio Drama School) in New York City. She is a recipient of that university's most prestigious award for "Excellence in Teaching."

As a performer, Ms. Thomas is an internationally acclaimed soprano whose work has been characterized as "ravishing in sound and magical in stage presence" (OPERA/London). International appearances have taken her to the opera houses of Cologne, Hamburg, Stuttgart, Paris, London, Dublin, Belfast, Mexico City, and Hong Kong. In the United States she has performed with the opera companies of New York City, Philadelphia, Santa Fe, Seattle,

Baltimore, Detroit, San Diego, Indianapolis, St. Louis, Louisville, Knoxville, Houston, Memphis, Grand Rapids, Nashville, Costa Mesa, New Jersey, El Paso, Syracuse, and Anchorage (among others). Concert engagements include performances with the Chicago Symphony, Cincinnati Symphony, and Indianapolis Symphony. Her repertoire features the heroines of La Traviata, Il Trovatore, Norma, Otello, Aida, Un Ballo in Maschera, Tosca, Madama Butterfly, Il Trittico, Macbeth, La Boheme, Faust, Cosi fan Tutte, Le Nozze di Figaro, Anna Bolena, Don Giovanni, Turandot, Dialoques des Carmelites, and Les Contes d'Hoffman. She has enjoyed a close collaboration with Dame Joan Sutherland and Maestro Richard Bonynge the latter with whom she recorded the title role in the Bohemian Girl for Decca Records. Other conductors and directors of renown with whom she has had the privilege of working are (among others) James Conlon, Carlo Rizzi, John Nelson, Michelangelo Veltri, John Crosby, Philippe Augin, Eduardo Muller, Maurizio Barbacini, Colin Grahm, Michael Hampe, Lotfi Mansouri, and John Pascoe,

Ms. Thomas is originally from North Carolina, and she has received her home state's Lifetime Achievement Award from the 4-H organization for her contributions to the arts. She works with the former Chair of the Joint Chiefs of Staff, General Henry Hugh Shelton, and serves on his Board of Advisors for a national leadership initiative.

James Conlon

One of today's preeminent conductors, James Conlon has cultivated a vast symphonic, operatic and choral repertoire, and developed enduring relationships with many of the world's most prestigious symphony orchestras and opera houses. Since his New York Philharmonic debut in 1974, Mr. Conlon has appeared as a guest conductor with virtually every major North American and European orchestra, and has appeared regularly at the Metropolitan Opera for a period of over thirty years.

Mr. Conlon is Music Director of the Los Angeles Opera; Music Director of the Ravinia Festival, the summer home of the Chicago Symphony Orchestra; and Music Director of the Cincinnati May Festival, where he celebrated his 30th Anniversary in May 2009. Mr. Conlon served as Principal Conductor of the Paris National Opera (1995–2004); General Music Director of the City of Cologne, Germany (1989–2002); and Music Director of the Rotterdam Philharmonic (1983–1991).

In an effort to raise public consciousness to the significance of works of composers whose lives and compositions were suppressed by the Nazi regime, Mr. Conlon has devoted himself to extensive programming of this music in North America and Europe. At both the Ravinia Festival and L.A. Opera, he continues to present works of these composers, including Alexander von Zemlinsky, Franz Schreker, Viktor Ullmann, Pavel Haas, Kurt Weill, Erich Wolfgang Korngold, Karl-Amadeus Hartmann, Erwin Schulhoff, Walther Braunfels and Ernest Krenek.

Mr. Conlon has recorded extensively for EMI, SONY Classical, ERATO, CAPRICCIO, and TELARC, for which he has received numerous citations. He has been featured on DVDs for DECCA, and has appeared in numerous television series on PBS. In 2009 Mr. Conlon won two Grammy

Awards (Best Classical Recording and Best Opera Album). Avidly devoted to education, he has been associated with the Juilliard School, Aspen Music Festival and Institute, Tanglewood and Steans Institutes. In his efforts to foster music education for the general public, he maintains an active public speaking schedule.

Other awards include the Music Institute of Chicago's Dushkin Award, the Medal of the American Liszt Society, and Italy's Premio Galileo 2000 Award. He received the Crystal Globe Award from the Anti-Defamation League (ADL) and is one of five recipients of the first Opera News Award for distinguished achievement in opera. He was awarded honorary Doctorates by The Juilliard School, Chapman University and Brandeis Universities. He received the Zemlinsky Prize for his efforts in bringing the composer's music to international attention. He was named an Officier de L'Ordre des Arts et des Lettres by the French Government in 1996, and in 2004 was promoted to Commander. In 2002, James Conlon received France's highest distinction, the Légion d'Honneur, from the then President of the Republic of France, Jacques Chirac.